DRUNK AS LORDS

ALSO BY RICHARD MURFF

Nonfiction
Pothole of the Gods:
On Holy War, Fake News & Other Ill-Advised Ideas

Fiction
Haint Punch
One Last Hour
Yellowcake

As Editor
Memphians

DRUNK AS LORDS:

THE WORLD IN ITS CUPS

BURNABY

For Maggie, Littlebit & Uncle Suitcase

CONTENTS

PREFACE:
WE'VE ALWAYS BEEN SOAKS

We've always been soaks, tipplers, boozers. Humans started drinking long before we even knew what it was, certainly before we knew how to make it. Bourbon porn on social media calls it "magic brown water." That may be overselling it, but the notion is an ancient one. Booze first appeared *gratis*, as if from the gods, and we took it for a magic that made *us* more interesting and *them* less scary. It strengthened bonds of affection and made discretion the lesser part of valor.

Humans developed a genetic mutation to process the stuff, then created societies built around it. The alchemists of old never cracked the nut of the turning lead into gold, but they kept improving booze to the point where it was used as money. So, grain into gold is worth *at least* a B+. Take a lap along the top shelf of any decent liquor store and you'll see that people are still turning grain and grape into gold. If you happen to be George Clooney, you can turn agave into gold. Heaps of the stuff. You might call it fool's gold, but it's gold nonetheless… and we're the fools. Despite learning its secrets, our mysterious fascination with booze has never really gone away. We've spent nearly all of human history thinking about, and trying to master, the sauce.

And yet, from our earliest ancestors to tomorrow's happy hour, there has been what the Greeks (no slouches at getting legless themselves) would have called our Achilles heel: That somewhere after the third round, just past the affection, warmth and *bonhomie* that magic juice will whisper in your ear, "Now it's time to tell them what you *really* think." This is ill-advised.

So, like the gods on Olympus, high protein diets, or those goons on Capitol Hill, booze giveth and booze taketh away.

You might think that a book like this would be addressed to the garden variety drunk, sleazy barfly, the terminally hep club goer, or even the under-the-radar "God and Elvis are everywhere, so I'm not *really* drinking alone" sort. It's not. None of those people need my help in ingesting enough psycho-actives to do something idiotic.

No, this book is for the one who doesn't drink a lot, just often. The collector of many well-lubricated stories, and the hero of a few others. The one who knows society has gotten just a little too uptight for its own good. And the way to ease these post-modern tensions just may be the oldest – well, second oldest – trick in the book. And as such thinks that the entire operation is worthy of a few style points.

In the words of the late Judge Noah S. "Soggy" Sweat, as delivered at King Edward Hotel in Jackson Mississippi in 1952 as the Mississippi State legislature was debating prohibition:

"My friends,

I had not intended to discuss this controversial subject at this particular time. However, I want you to know that I do not shun controversy. On the contrary, I will take a stand on any issue at any time, regardless of how fraught with controversy it might be. You have asked me how I feel about whiskey. All right, here is how I feel about whiskey.

"If when you say whiskey you mean the devil's brew, the poison scourge, the bloody monster, that defiles innocence, dethrones reason, destroys the home, creates misery and poverty, yea, literally takes the bread from the mouths of little children; if you mean the evil drink that topples the Christian man and woman from the pinnacle of righteous, gracious living into the bottomless pit of degradation, and despair, and shame and helplessness, and hopelessness, then certainly I am against it.

"But;

"If when you say whiskey you mean the oil of conversation, the philosophic wine, the ale that is consumed when good fellows get together, that puts a song in their hearts and laughter on their lips, and the warm glow of contentment in their eyes; if you mean Christmas cheer; if you mean the stimulating drink that puts the spring in the old gentleman's step on a frosty, crispy morning; if you mean the drink which enables a man to magnify his joy, and his happiness, and to forget, if only for a little while, life's great tragedies, and heartaches, and sorrows; if you mean that drink, the sale of which pours into our treasuries untold millions of dollars, which are used to provide tender care for our little crippled children, our blind, our deaf, our dumb, our pitiful aged and infirm; to build highways and hospitals and schools, then certainly I am for it.

"This is my stand. I will not retreat from it. I will not compromise."

PART ONE:
IN THE BEGINNING

DRUNK MONKEYS

VAPOR TRAILS

YE GODS!

LEGLESS PHILOSOPHERS

CRAPULUS SUM

DRUNK MONKEYS

If nothing else, booze is natural. Just leave fruit around to get breathed on by some air-borne yeast and rot *just so* and it will ferment, turning that sweet sugar into alcohol. For Ben Franklin, this was all the proof he needed that God loved us and wanted us to be happy. To get all Oprah about it, this might just be proof that the universe really does provide us with everything we need. The rub is that the universe doesn't produce everything that we want. And what we've wanted, since we literally came out of the trees, was to get gassed.

That's saying something because those trees which our earliest forebears called home provided fresh food and protection from anything that couldn't climb a tree. The fresh fruit hanging up there was lovely and conveniently above the heads of most of what was trying to eat you. Gravity was a bit tricky, but it made waste disposal was a snap (more on that later). Why would anyone bother going downstairs, as it were? It turns out there was at least one reason to climb down to *terra firma*: When the gravitationally challenged over-ripe fruit fell from the trees, nature took over. The chemical process that came next was not, in retrospect, very complicated, but it did take most of human history to sort out.

It's literally called the Drunken Monkey theory, and it posits that, like teenagers going to lousy neighborhood in search of a gas station that doesn't card, early humans came down from the trees sniffing around for booze. It's not universally accepted but, as we'll see, it does ring a lot of bells.

Over-ripe fruit has lots of sugar, meaning lots of easy calories. Eventually this tasty, waterlogged sugar bomb will drop from its perch and fall to the earth. The impact most likely split the fruit's protective skin. This was important, because humans aren't the only ones who like sugar. Tiny one-celled plants called yeasts live for the stuff. When they land in some they suck it up and – there is no good way to say this – *excrete* alcohol. We call this fermentation because it took millennia to figure out what was going on and, when we did, "yeast piss" sounded very unappealing.

Alcohol, it turns out has some evolutionary purpose above and beyond just feelin' groovy. It triggers the sensation of hunger in humans, causing us to eat more calories than we need *at the time* for future storage. Having a drink before dinner, or even as dinner, was an evolutionary nudge that kept our caloric savings account well-padded. It still does.

The theory follows that we developed a "nose" for alcohol because it led us to the extra sugar and calories needed for that favorite pastime of early humans: Running for dear life from everything that was trying to kill you. Understand also that for 99.999% of human existence, the world was such a hairy and violent place that the mere ability to get fat was a huge plus in terms of survival. In short, having a store of excess calories got you laid. That, if we're going to be honest, is the end-game for any evolutionary adaptation.

Unfortunately for modern drinkers, evolution moves far slower than Instagram. The knock-on effect was that some God-only-knows how many years later the taste of smell of alcohol still triggers our appetite and causes us to eat too much, knowing full well that love handles have gone out of fashion.

All well and good, but you may have noticed that alcohol will do more than compel you to start picking off your date's plate. It'll get you sideways if you aren't careful. Although what evolutionary purpose the rambling, pointless run-on sentence serves is beyond me. Some biologists reckon that about 10 million years ago, we developed a genetic mutation that caused us to produce an enzyme (ADH4 – and that's really *all* I know about that) to help us better process the alcohol we craved. Well, at least better than a chimpanzee.

That strange mutation had a clear impact. Primates – apes, chimpanzees, teenagers – are essentially social animals. For humans, coming out of the trees the way we did, social groups became a lot more important because there is safety in numbers. If you are part of a pack, then a short turn of bad luck may not prove fatal because you've got family and friends to help out. Of course, it's not just your charming personality, but the fact that they know that you'll help them through a bad turn too. They have faith in you for the same reason you have faith in them – because whoever doesn't hold the bargain gets socially banished. Living off the grid in some cabin may seem like a good idea, but only to someone lucky enough to have lived in relative luxury for long enough to get bored with it. In those days it meant that only with an unbroken streak of fantastic, unsustainable, luck was it possible to live into the next financial quarter. Even a drunk monkey can calculate those odds.

So, the pack provided safety, while a nose for alcohol led us to sugary calories that we shared with the gang and they shared with us. The alcohol, once we'd developed the right enzyme, didn't slap us around too mightily anymore. The mutation allowed us to socialize the effects of booze. It made us feel all fuzzy within the group and we got all "I love you, Man" and "She's my BFF, *amirite!*" And the gang grew tighter. At this distance, there is no way to prove that events unfolded exactly this way, but anyone who ever pledged a sorority or fraternity has likely lived through a live action example of this sort of foolishness. We've been doing this for a very long time and evolutionarily formed habits are very, very hard to break.

The arrangement worked so well that early humans were able to invent something of a game changer: Old people. The earliest evidence of hand tools seems to coincide with the existence of teeth from old people – and by that I mean anyone who has reached about the age of 30. Granted, these thirtysomethings and their novel impulse control were still something of a rarity those days, but there were enough of them around to say lame things like "Now, I wouldn't do that if I were you."

All of these developments led to more humanoids loitering about. This was progress, you understand, but it presented a tricky problem. While nature does produce alcohol naturally, it doesn't produce that much of it by accident. Not enough to get really pie-eyed, at any rate.

I gnorance and stupidity are not the same thing. We all start out ignorant, and while a large part of the population chooses to stay that way, you *can* do something about it. Just asking questions and then shutting your trap while you listen will singlehandedly correct most ignorance. There isn't much you can do about stupidity.

Early humans weren't stupid, they just didn't have the benefit of 300,000 years of trial and error and productivity reports to help them out. They were dealing with a complete dearth of the accumulated knowledge that we take entirely for granted. It's one thing to learn your ABCs or your multiplication tables, it is a different magnitude all together to actually invent writing and mathematics. The safe bet is that our ancestors, while ignorant, were a lot smarter than us. They had to be, their entire world was trial and error. And observation.

Fortunately, booze isn't that hard to make if your standards are low enough. Learning the trick actually gets fairly simple if you focus on the "what just happened?" rather that the "why did that happen?" And probably what happened, aside from sniffing out over-ripe melons, was a dead tree that had been colonized by bees was knocked over in a storm and the cavity filled with water in roughly the right ratio to the honeycomb inside, add a little invisible airborne yeast and sit there long enough to start to do its thing. Presto! The universe has provided you with a tree trunk of mead. Sure, to the   modern drinker the final product lacked finesse, but these were people who shoved their faces in ponds and creeks every time they got thirsty.

Along strolls a pair of early humans with an idea to get up to something that's even easier to figure than making booze. On their walk, they smell a dead tree full of sweet, honey-water and dunk their faces into it for a long slurp. It tastes good, they take another. Then another. What happens next is both groovy and scrumptious. We're sitting on the accumulated knowledge of humanity – so we can make an educated guess. All these two know is that they wandered up to a tree full of waterlogged honey and realized that it made them taller, smarter and just a bit less gross.*

Alas, a log full of mead just lying about is a rare thing. Early humans reckoned the *Why* was fairly unknowable and living in a global community garden that is trying to kill you as a baseline activity, it is also irrelevant. You just want to know *What* is trying to kill you and if you're a real intellectual, perhaps *How* fate plans to execute the maneuver. When it came to booze, people focused on the *What* so they could do it again. With a little of reverse engineering they figured out how to create their own.

With fruit, especially grapes, you don't even need to add water like you do with honeycomb. All you need is a container that is mostly watertight. The oldest evidence of pottery, found in what is now the Czech Republic, dates from 29,000 to 25,000 BC, and in China as far back as 18,000

---

* Don't you sneer. And after ten millennia of evidence to the contrary, most of us fall for this one every-time we hoist a few.

BC. Now, this was earthenware pottery, which is porous but it was good enough. Excavations in southern Europe have revealed large caches of grape seeds, which is telling. If these people were walking around eating grapes and spitting the seeds out, they'd be scattered all over the place. Even if grapes had been gathered for communal eating, the seeds would still be in all over the camp site. Big piles of grape seeds suggest that they were left in the pot to dissolve, or more specifically, the make wine.

And that is pretty much all they knew about it.

There was an invisible third party actor that early producers couldn't see, didn't know was there and so certainly couldn't fathom its role in making booze. That hardly mattered because in nature you can't avoid yeast. It's all over the place and so small that it gets moved about every-time the wind blows. Early humans didn't know or care. What they had sorted out was pretty straightforward: Put fruit in a bowl, maybe add water or maybe don't, and then leave it alone. They didn't know *Why* it happened, or even *How*, they just knew that something was happening. Like magic.

So, the theory goes, we came out of the trees, got drunk, did what came natural. The population grew and it was only a matter of time before packs grew into clans and clans into tribes and eventually humans started to engineer something we'd call society.

What society did was drastically outpace nature's ability to just hand the sauce out willy-nilly and free of charge. Humans reckoned that, if we were going to be humans, we needed to take matters into our own hands. Like the early log o' mead, the standards were pretty damned low. Still, the world was at least slightly less dangerous within the group, and the group tended to bond with alcohol.

There is a very good reason for this, best put by Kingsley Amis in his classic *Everyday Drinking*:

> The human race has not devised any way of dissolving barriers, getting to know the other chap fast, breaking the ice, that is one tenth as handy and efficient as letting you and the other chap, or chaps, cease to be totally sober at about the same rate in agreeable surroundings.

Drunk as Lords

VAPOR TRAILS

One of the oldest known human structures still in existence is in Göbekli Tepe in Turkey, and dates from about 9,000 BC. Located in some agreeable surrounding at the foothills of the Taurus Mountains, it is a raised mound situated on a limestone plateau that was surrounded – at the time – by an open grassland of wild cereals. The structure is centrally located among some semi-permanent settlements, but it doesn't appear to be a shelter itself because it didn't have a roof. Yet it clearly took a group effort to build the thing as some of the stone slabs used weigh some 16 tons. This was not a "camp" for surrounding nomads, although it may have been a meeting place.

Archeologist Klaus Schmidt called it a "Cathedral on a Hill" suggesting that it drew people from up to 90 miles away. Fair enough, he certainly looked into it further than I did. There are also several stone cisterns, about 40 gallons each, carved into the limestone bedrock. Excavations suggest that they were connected to a rainwater harvesting system. They don't, however seem to be precisely for drinking water. The cisterns contain traces of a chemical called oxalate, which created by mixing barley and water.

Who knows why anyone does anything? After all our evolution, therapy and supportive hashtags, we can't even fully comprehend why we eat a piece of cheesecake ten minutes after deciding that we are too full to walk. The average grad-student can't fathom the mind of ancients born when The Beatles were still a thing. So how can we divine the motives of ancient foreigners from 11,000 years ago? The short answer is that we can't. Still, even from this distance it looks like it was a place to meet, have a drink and cease to be totally sober at about the same rate.

It is around this time that wine shows up in the Transcaucasia – straddling the Caucasus Mountains where extreme eastern Europe touches extreme western Asia – as an important part of their culture. Both of which support the plausible but boozy theory of civilization that we didn't create agriculture to feed ourselves but to have something to drink with it. There is something to this: The global population at this point was roughly between one and ten million. For reference and to spilt the difference, the 2020 population of the (mostly empty) state of Alabama is about five million. Spread those people out here and there over the entire planet, one big community garden on autopilot, and there is really no good reason to sit down and decide to become a farmer. The earth was just giving the stuff away. Granted the fully weaponized flora and fauna kept you on your toes, but eating enough to stay upright didn't require too much effort.* To get enough booze to get your swerve on

---

* Even if becoming a proper chubs was fairly aspirational.

with other humans in way that made them less likely to try to kill you, however, needed some engineering.

To avoid having some aggrieved undergraduate and their deranged associate professor righteously berate me for not being inclusive enough, let me point out the practical reality of this sort of historical research. History is really just a great deal of groping around for vapor trails in the dark, prehistory even moreso. The reason that we head to the Levant and the Near East so often when discussing the dawn of civilization is because that's where so much of the surviving evidence is. *Surviving* being the key word here. Abandon a stone structure in an arid climate, and barring some "cultural revolution" where some ass attempts to rewrite history by destroying it, and parts of it be there 12,000 years later. Conveniently located so an intrepid archeologist can justify a lump of grant money. Abandon a wooden structure in a humid place, dump a lot of rain on it, and it will be erased fairly quickly. In some cases, like South America or Southeast Asia, in as little as a generation or two.

As early as 7,000 BC there is clear evidence of wine being made in large(ish) quantities in China. These are the oldest such vessels that modern people have found. For all we know they could have been fifth generation winemaking technology. We can assume that without GPS, cars or shoes, that the people in Turkey and those in China probably didn't know each other well enough to swap ideas. It is in Henan province in northern central China, where the first *identifiable* alcoholic was produced. Again, identifiable being the key word. While the recipe card has been lost, chemical analysis reveals that it was a blend of fermented honey (mead, again), probably grapes and a beer made from rice. Don't sneer, Budweiser and Coors both use heaps of rice in their brew. Rice beer isn't quite as simple as the barely kind, requiring the grains to be chewed prior to fermentation in to convert the starch into sugar.*

So across this inclusive world of ours we've been drinking together for along time. Even when we were far apart. And why not? It's pleasant, and good for you – up to a point. It's good for society – again, up to a point.

It does, however, have a curious knock-on effect: Wherever you are, bonding with alcohol tends to trigger the asking of unknowable questions. Our rumination goes from the immediately practical *How the hell did that cave bear get in here!?!* to the decidedly more unwieldy *Why are we here?* Despite being utterly unknowable, the one you are drinking with – be it wizened sage or blockhead drinking buddy – is likely to give you a really big answer.

We just can't help it.

---

* I have it on good authority from the people Budweiser and Coors that their modern process is less *yetchy*.

T he yeast that made all of this possible wouldn't be identified until the 18th century. That unknowability, combined with a mild psycho-active quality, is likely the reason that the stuff was universally considered a gift from the gods. Or Goddess, most likely.

The theory is that prior to society getting complex enough to support a lot of division of labor, early humans, as far as they thought about it, were vaguely monotheistic. Crude images of a big bellied, big breasted Mother Nature sort crops up across a great many unconnected people.

Regardless who they thought was running the place, that unknowable magic of turning fruit into wine or barley into beer was our connection to the divine. It is also what separates us from the animals.

A creation myth from western Africa has a creator telling some lady monkeys to come down from the trees, and shows them how to make porridge and brew beer. And as they get to work, their fur falls away and tails drop from their behinds. What this myth tells us is that it is the ability to make our own food and booze is what makes us human.

It also tells us that a woman's work is never done.

YE GODS!

So, people, being people, figured out the mystery of making babies a lot faster than making booze; and we can safely assume that it was the ladies who first sorted the math on that one. That the earliest creation myths were couched in sex is entirely logical, because that's where life starts. Less obvious is how many of these tales involve the gods getting hammered. Given the hairy unpredictably of life, as well as the perceived connection of booze and the divine, maybe it's not that strange. More practically, early humans just came up with the stories after a couple of rounds of the sauce. However it happened, drunkenness got conflated with sex and creation myths in early attempts at the *Why*.

As society became more complex and individual roles broke up into more specialized labor, early humans imagined the unknowable the same way. A vaguely monotheistic Mother Goddess started to split into goddesses and gods with specialized jobs and tasks. The division of labor in society led to greater efficiencies as well as a more complex society with more defined hierarchy. As it did, the gods people envisioned became more complex as well. The deities, like their chiefs and kings and queens, were petty, selfish and violent. Sure, they might do you the odd favor here and there, for a price, but there seems to be no strong feeling that the gods loved the humanity they created. Or even liked it that much.

In the ancient city of Ur, in that fertile crescent between the Tigris and Euphrates rivers (read: modern Iraq) they had a goddess of beer: Ninkasi. And she was a goddess – their word for tavern-keeper was a feminine noun. We know this because by about 3,200 BC the people living there, the Sumerians, had developed writing and, strange for a barter economy with no hard currency, accountancy and somewhat standardized pricing. They traded the obvious gold, silver and spices, but also livestock, sex, measures of barley and beer. Although, the beer in question looked more like warm, watery oatmeal to modern eyes. All the solid crud floated to the top, so you drank it with a long straw where the stuff was both cooler and less chunky.* Humanity's standards were still pretty low, but it would get you sideways if you really needed it too.

Getting really gassed wasn't anything that was considered unholy. Ill-advised, sure, but nothing as sinful as, say, laughing at the local priest's funny hat. To illustrate this, the Sumerians managed to work some drunken foolishness of the gods into their creation myth. Their version involves the goddess of sex, Inana, and the god of wisdom, Enki, getting into a drinking game which Enki promptly loses when he passes out. One might draw the inference that both sex

---

* My brother and I both brewed a beer called Murffbrau in college. Its motto was "It's not real beer unless you can chew it." My brother still brews, but now Murffbrau is feature in dinners at a local B&B. It's no longer chunky.

and drinking trumps wisdom. One would be right on both counts. Inana then steals Enki's wisdom and takes it down to Earth. While down on *terra firma*, she then has sex with some feral half-man named Enkidu and afterwards gets the boy drunk. And this is what makes him fully human: Drinking and sex.

The creation myth of the Yoruba in western Africa isn't about Olurun, the god of the heavens, actually getting it on with Olukun, goddess of the watery abyss. It's more about them wanting to get it on. They must have at some point, because their son, Obatala, wants to unite them by creating the Earth to connect the heavens and the oceans. He tells Olurun about the plan, and dad is delighted at the thought of seeing the old girl from the watery abyss again. Dad advised the boy to seek advice from his brother, Orunmilla, a master of divination. Orunmilla makes a list of seven items Obatala will need, and he sets off terraforming.

After much toil and turmoil, Obatala had only two unused items: a black cat and a palm seed, from which he grew a fine tree under which he and the cat spent their time lounging. After the cat pointed out the joys of palm wine, Obatala found himself a little distracted and didn't follow through with his final task, which was to fill the land with living things.

After a night of drinking and dancing, Obatala fell into a drunken stupor.* While he slumbered, his brother Orunmila

---

* With the cat? Even for the divine, the standards of entertainment were pretty low.

descended to Earth, and set about creating life; all that swims through the water, crawls on the land, or flies through air can thank Orunmila, as Obatala was sleeping one off.

Obatala woke up shocked. He ascended to the heavens and confronted his father, who shrugged off his anger. However, as a peace gesture, Dad pointed out that Ournmila had failed to create humanity, and offered that job to Obatala as a consolation prize. The boy returned to the Earth to create human beings. Unfortunately, he was still a little gassed.* And thus, all human maladies, misfortunes and mishaps can be explained by the day the gods drank too much.

Or as they still say in those parts, "Don't blame us, god was drunk when he made us this way."

The Biblical story of Noah isn't strictly an origin story, but one of the near-miss *destruction of all mankind* cautionary tales that seem to crop up near the dawn of civilization. After getting an alarming early weather report, Noah builds an ark and floats around on floodwaters for 40 days. The rest of humanity drowns like a sack of unwanted kittens and Noah contemplates the fortune to be made on livestock futures. Eventually the waters recede and the ark comes to rest on Mount Ararat (in modern Turkey) where, reportedly, he planted vines and got drunk.

All of which could be written off as a complete myth except that in 2010, evidence was discovered of a winery dating back to 4,000 BC in the neighborhood we'd call the

---

* Palm wine, what are you gonna do?

Transcaucus. And it doesn't appear that the wine was entirely for local consumption either.

Upriver from Ur, and downriver from the Ararat Valley, was the next big thing in civilization, Babylon (about 50 miles from modern Bagdad). There King Hammurabi wrote his famous law codes, one of which stipulated the loss of a hand as penalty for selling bad wine. Despite Hammurabi's carrying on about protecting the weak from the strong, bad wine really was a rich guy problem.

Further to the south, the Egyptians also drank wine brought in from the Ararat Valley region. And like the Babylonians, it was a rich man's drink. The way the Egyptians had it figured, wine was a gift from the god Osiris. As a divinity, Osiris had a wide brief: the god of agriculture, fertility, the afterlife, death and resurrection, and vegetation. This may not be as random as it sounds – the common thread is regeneration, rebirth and a snort of something that will give you second wind.

Wine was used in medicines, perfumes and, of course to get sideways. That all social and economic levels of ancient Egyptians drank all the time is pretty evident. That all levels were gassed all the time is not. The place was awash in pomegranate, date and palm wine, but what the upper-classes wanted was wine of the vine.

What the lower classes got was beer. Lower in alcohol and heartier to drink, again, don't think Guinness, but oatmeal under the influence. In a world before refrigeration, painkillers, antibiotics and plastic wrap, the stuff was actually good for you. In the 1990's scientists found traces of tetracycline in the Nile Valley mummies; curious as tetracycline wasn't invented until 1953. It turns out that the way the Egyptians made beer produced not only a mild buzz, but an antibiotic as well. They didn't know this of course, but they knew something was up with the stuff because with it they lived longer and felt better. Like everyone else, they thought it was from the gods. And given the way they envisioned that bunch, they really wanted to remain in divine favor. Their version of humanity's near-miss *destruction of all mankind* cautionary tale that was decidedly more harrowing than the Noah story.

Ra was the Egyptian sun god. If you've ever been to North Africa, the sun does tend to dominate things, and this made Ra pretty much top dog. I suppose that the sun-god doesn't have much to do at night, so he was all alone and decided to take matters into his own hand. The upshot is that he popped off after a wank and got himself in the open mouth by accident – thus creating the world. I really don't know what to make of that, so let's keep going, shall we?

Like in the Noah story, Ra decided that the humanity he'd created by accident was getting a little too uppity. Given the start they had, who could be surprised? At any rate, as gods did in the olden days, he decided to kill the ungrateful humans off. He called a goddess from the south named Hathor to do the deed. Sometimes she's Ra's mother, and sometimes his daughter, but she was considered the patroness of sex and the embodiment of Egyptian femininity. Which is why what happened next is so alarming.

She leaned into her brief with such unbridled enthusiasm that it startled even Ra himself. He tried to stop her, he really did, but Hathor had gone full rampage. So Ra whipped up some thousands of kegs of beer – all dyed red – and spilled it all over the place. Hathor mistook it for the buckets human blood she'd split and, because she was into *that scene*, lapped it up. Then she rather lost the thread of things and took a nap. Humanity was saved.

With a role model like that, the ancient Egyptians leaned into drinking and sex like Hathor on a rampage. They bragged about both constantly. It's hard to tell how widespread this was: Consider 30th century anthropologists taking a long look at surviving *Real Housewives* reels and thinking that is an accurate picture of 21st century America. The reality television level of debauch was probably a rich thing. The strange Festival of Drunkenness – in honor of genocidal Hathor – was very much an elite get-together and likely a wine crowd. Like beer, ancient wine is probably not what you are currently imagining.

Originally imported from Ararat or surrounding regions some 900 miles away, by 2,500 BC royalty and the aristocrats had their own vineyards, but it wasn't for resale. Evidence suggested that it was mostly red, or at least started that way. Without modern bottling, it went off pretty quickly so it was fortified with tree resin as a preservative. What we are looking at is a thick, sticky wine that tasted more like tree sap the longer it sat. It turned brown. To counteract both the bitter taste and the fact that it was rapidly turning to vinegar, they added spices and honey, which may have improved the taste, but did nothing to thin it out.

The Festival of Drunkenness started simply enough with all the beautiful people dressed to the nines for a little late afternoon day-drinking, then following a procession into the forecourt Temple of Hathor. At this point it wasn't that much different from the Met Gala. Then they really started to hit the sauce. I don't mean in a Met Gala hedge against social anxiety, but Studio 54 sex-bridge sort of foolishness. These people were getting weapons-grade and they were doing it with intent. Enough to where the infamous "boot-and-rally" wasn't just one of those things that happens, it was the point. The high priests throwing the hootenanny spiked the wine with herbs designed to make you hurl before you went comatose. This was important because you wanted to stay conscious enough for the orgy.

Never having attended an orgy myself, I'm not entirely clear on the etiquette, but there seems to be no sense of "dance with the one who brought you" at these events. There certainly wasn't in the temple of Hathor. The whole point of the exercise was to cover as much ground as possible.

After all that, everyone passed out in a big, sweaty, probably very sticky, heap. After not nearly enough time to sleep the rager off, the priests came in and changed around statues and *object d'art* to convince the confused revelers on waking that a miracle had happened.

Here the Egyptian put their own twist on the whole *booze as a window to the divine* business. Most ancients used the euphoria of drunkenness to await an epiphany from the gods. The Egyptians used the slow-witted, grumpy confusion of the vaguely drunk hangover for the blessed reveal.

I won't even drink a bourbon & coke because that much sugar in a great way to get a head-splitting hangover. Tree sap and honey? In your red wine? Being woken up while still half-drunk in a world without air-conditioning, aspirin or Gatorade? But lots of vomit? Personally, I'd be more inclined to see 900 angry devils than god. Of course, given that the entire exercise was in honor of Hathor, who could tell the difference?

By this point in human history, the *How* of baby making was old hat. So no one was really surprised when these fancy ladies turned up pregnant after the orgy. When these gals looked at each other and said, "Ra only knows who the father is!" they meant it, literally. Was the husband jealous? Heavens no! The way they had things sorted, it was a divine blessing: After all that semi-anonymous sex in a room with no ventilation, but lots of particularly viscous, sap-flavored vomit, weren't we blessed that the little lady got knocked up by a goddess… a divine female. Well, it probably made more sense if you were hungover. At any rate, a little tapper conceived while Hathor looked on was a shoo in for the priesthood – which, we can surmise, was a lot livelier that it is today.

And all Christians get is a barn floating in the rain for 40 days and Adam and Eve in a vegetable bikini.

"STAND UP PHILOSOPHER."

"A WHAT?"

"STAND UP PHILOSOPHER. I COALESCE
THE VAPOR OF HUMAN EXPERIENCE INTO A
VIABLE AND LOGICAL COMPREHENSION."

"OH... A BULLSHIT ARTIST!"

MEL BROOKS
HISTORY OF THE WORLD, PART I

LEGLESS PHILOSOPHERS

I'm not suggesting that the Greeks were the first to make the leap from *What* and *How* to the more philosophical *Why*. They do, however, seem to be the first to turn it into a national pastime. And they were very good at it. Although "nation" is the wrong word for it: Athens was a city-state in Greece, and so was Sparta, but were as culturally similar as Vicksburg, Mississippi is to Portland, Oregon.

In Athens, they were always asking each other why the seasons changed, or why did Erasthos just keel over dead in that interesting way? It's a good thing too, because despite their best efforts to the contrary, the Athenians invented democracy, the seeds of economics, education, modern mathematics, engineering and literature and many of the swell things we associate with civilization.

Of course, civilization has its downsides as well. Nomadic people didn't have to deal with their own sewage. In a world with a global population of ten million you can wander around popping a squat with environmental impunity because the ecosystem takes it in stride. Jack the numbers up enough to build a proper city where all those people stay in one place and the crap really starts to stack up.

Or more precisely, it seeps into the water. One of Mother Nature's cruelest jokes is that any place with enough people to built a real city likely had fouled well-water. The clever and inquisitive Greeks figured out, like a lot of ancient cultures, that drinking water was a safer if you poured some wine into it.

In the interests of putting things into a wider context, spiking your water wasn't the only option. It was just simple, fun and widely available. For one thing, bumpkins out in the country weren't faced with this particular problem (though they faced a host of others). Reclaiming rainwater was both wide-spread and fairly obvious as solutions go, but a steady supply was always an issue in an arid climate.

By 400 BC there is evidence that the Phoenicians in the Levant were using charcoal filters to clean their water. They were a wide-ranging seafaring people, and routinely charred the inside of water barrels to retard contamination. The technology spread through Africa and Greece, where they were also experimenting with distillation to desalinate sea-water.

Even the less clever Spartans drank wine all the time. Since they were fundamentally bad conversationalists, however, they made sure no one had any fun drinking. The Spartans hadn't always been that way. At one point in their history, the culture had been so hedonistic that it essentially collapsed. What came out of the ruin was a society determined not to let it happen again. The Spartan culture we think we know is a society-wide version of the pledge a fella makes when he wakes up, can't remember the last week and notes his wrecked car in the lawn as he's being served papers and realizes that he is short one wife, both kids and the dog.

The Spartans, for all their macho image, were terrified of their impulses. It made them very pious in their own demented way. They thought that getting sideways was unmanly and the Spartans were all about the manly. Although they had a funny way of defining it: Pedophilia, for instance, was considered quite manly, and for the macho man about town an oiled boy-toy was *de rigueur,* so what the hell? It's hard to say whether a bender would have improved their general temperament or made it worse. As tightly wound as they were, they certainly could have used the odd cocktail hour to take the edge off. On the other hand, they were probably not very fun drunks. To warn the kiddos off the sauce, Spartan parents would force-feed their slaves enough uncut wine to get degradingly pole-axed as a sort of horrifying live-action *Scared Straight* cautionary tale.

The more laid-back Athenians of Attica preferred to think big thoughts.* It didn't seem to matter if you framed your big thoughts in religion or philosophy – apparently you still had to get drunk to get there. As the fourth century BC Greek play write Aristophanes wrote: "Quickly, bring me a beaker of wine so that I may whet my mind and say something clever."

After a lifetime of my own trial and error experiments, I'm not sure that last bit holds, but the Greeks believed it.

---

* To be fair they were all about sex with middle-schoolers as well, they were just more philosophical about it.

Enter the symposium – the word literally means "drinking together." It was both educational and social, a sort of hybrid high-minded debate/drinking club. A dozen or so fellas, and they would always be fellas, got together to discuss big ideas. The wine was mixed in a large jar called a *krater* with about two parts unpolluted sea-water, the deeper the better, to wine. The wine we are talking about was so harsh that the salty seawater actually improved the flavor, as well as cut the tree resin which was also being used pretty liberally.

The wine wasn't just to break the ice and get the intellectual juices flowing *a la* Kingsley Amis; the whole point was to get absolutely plastered. It wasn't exactly a free-for-all, guests drank when the host did, so he could somewhat control the proceedings. The word drink is probably conveying the wrong image . This wasn't a swirl it around in the stemware before sipping sort of affair, these people were quaffing the stuff. This being Athens, in theory it was a meeting of free equals but the host acted as the pace-car: He could go nuts, but he was drinking just as much as his peers.

Even from this distance, you can pick out some male bravado, albeit the intellectual sort. Plato, who was always thinking too much, said that drunkenness not only tested a man's self-control, but trained it. He likened self-control to bravery, and bravery could only be taught by surviving harrowing events. What you couldn't do is test your bravery sitting on mom's cushy lap. Likewise, if you were clear-eyed and sober, it was fairly easy to remain in control of your faculties.* Knocking back bowls of wine and seawater while your peers demanded you hold forth on this big idea or that one was like battle for the senses. The more you drank, the more a man could test – and expand – the limits of his self-control. The way the Greeks had it figured, the ideal fellow was one you could drink a ton and never get swirly. Supposedly the famed Socrates was like this, and we're still talking about that guy.

It wasn't all philosophy, there was a whole pantheon divinities. Like most religions of antiquity, the Greeks had what only can be called a "professional" relationship with the gods. There were the well-ordered cities of man, the unknowable heights of heaven, and the chaotic wilderness as sort of porous membrane between the two worlds. Alcohol was a gift but less the bounty of loving gods and more along the lines of your celestial insurance agent sending you a desk calendar. Still, a gift is a gift. If you got crossways with Hera or Apollo, you politely fired them. No one wants to be godless, so you slaughtered a cow or slave, or had sex with them, and there you were, you had another god on retainer. It isn't like you lacked choices, they had enough gods for a reality show – with spinoffs.

Like music or contemporary politics, what god you prayed to said a lot about you, what we'd call a lifestyle choice. So as the god of wine, Dionysus was popular after a manner, but not very well regarded. Sort of like that drunk cousin whom you genuinely like, but aren't about to loan any

---

* Debatable.

money to. Even Dionysus's beautiful, vain, and practical stepmother, Hera, wasn't impressed. She was a bit of a twat by all reports and cast Dionysus out to wander the earth in a fog of madness. Somehow our wandering nut-job fell in with one of the lesser goddess, Rhea, who cured his madness and taught him how to make wine. Perhaps he wasn't entirely cured because he decided that India, of all places, might be a good spot to throw a party. In some tellings, Dionysus is actually from India… or Persia. Some place that isn't Greece and the Greeks thought that was worth reminding everyone.

Having had all the fun he could stand abroad, the young god set off for home* in search of a job. On the way back to Greece, he started pandering for worshipers along Asia Minor. The prospecting didn't go so well, the locals didn't entirely like the look of the boy. For one thing, he wore a funny looking head-band, or *mitra*, that was a cure for the incessant hangover from which the god of wine and merriment was always suffering. There was also the issue of his reputation: Wild abandon followed him everywhere he went like that cousin with the Jell-O shots.

Local princes weren't entirely sure that they wanted Dionysus and his heady wine, unnatural orgies and anti-hangover hat hanging around being disruptive. Imagine trying convince the Rotary Club of Provo, Utah to take Mardi Gras off the hands of New Orleans. Running the

---

* Strictly speaking, if he was a foreigner, his home wouldn't be Greece, but there we are.

anti-Dionysus campaign was King Pentheus and a fella named Lycurgus.*

It wasn't all bad press, the myth continues: Many seemed taken with his good looks and some, a little too taken. While sitting on the seashore, nursing another hangover, he caught the eye of a boat load of sailors who wanted a piece of *that*. That back-door foolishness wasn't Dionysus's cup of tea, so he turned the sailors into dolphins. Dionysus was always doing things like this; not being a tease, but turning folks into animals. Not only was it a great party trick, there was a moral as well – mess with the sauce too much and you'll turn into a beast. Great lesson, but there is a sizable hole in the plot: If Dionysus could transform people into livestock, why he was suffering all those hangovers? Why he didn't turn one of them into a classical age Alka-Seltzer and a bloody mary combo is one of the great mysteries of badly organized religion.

All the resistance was getting the boy down. He couldn't reckon why people wouldn't worship him. It wasn't like he was preaching austere self-sacrifice, his was a hep, good natured cult. He did have an entourage of wild women as followers called *maenads*, who lived in the mountains, got wildly drunk as a form of worship and were very cavalier about clothing. It's unknown whether these gals actually existed or were just something thought up by the guys. The ancient world's equivalent of what boys still think goes on in sorority houses. Fantasy or not, their sisters did in fact show

---

* Whom, I think, won a Grammy last year.

up in Rome a few generations later to wreak very real havoc. More on *that* later.

Dionysus discovered his niche when he found his way to Mount Olympus and pestered his dad for a job. Working for Zeus, he was promoted to being god of other things, like god of vegetation and warm moisture. Yes, the Greeks had a god of warm moisture…the god of steam or if you will, humidity.

At least that's the way the priests told it.

Back in reality, a Festival of Dionysus was thrown by a cult that was decidedly not in the "sinners in the hands of an angry god" camp. This was a loopy affair intended to ease the present misery of being alive through wild abandon. Even the slaves went free for the festival. Which might not have been as gracious as it seems, because someone had to clean up the mess when it was all over.

Like in the forecourt of Hathor, the priests were stage-managing the miracles. At one of Dionysus's temples there was even a water-into-wine "miracle" performed on cue. The temple fountain had a secret passage in its the bowels where a high priest could shut off the water course feeding the fountain and pour wine down it instead.

As long as you didn't think too hard about it, it must have seemed dazzling. Outside the temple there was music and suggestive dancing all in honor of a huge phallus that was to be…ah hem…erected at the focal point of the festival. How could it not be the focal point? How often to you see a forty-foot boner with girls dressed as nymphs and men not dressed at all crawling over it?

Icarus, soaring above as he glided too close to the sun, must have thought that the horny countryside had gotten a really colorful case of the crabs.

G reece was the first culture around where they thought having the *demos* run everything was a clever idea. They were also the first where the common *demos* drank wine. There isn't much evidence that the Greeks had what we'd call beer, but the wine flowed both red and white and all of it was full of sap. They flavored it with honey and spices and used the stuff as medicine, laxatives, water disinfectant, and to just tie one on. Being a very vivi-centric culture, they even pioneered the drying out of grapes to concentrate the sugars and then turn the raisins into wine. The higher sugar led to higher alcohol which led to a long shelf life which led to more chewy wine.

The Festival of Dionysus and the symposium aside, it wasn't just a big wine and saltwater free for all. Even philosophical Athenians could see that, yes, alcohol was divine, but it was also a slippery slope. They thought that the stuff could actually drive you insane. True, this wasn't the sort of thing that was likely to happen in the environs of the upper-class boys club symposium, but wine could get out of hand and turn you into an animal.

We know that the Greeks had the technical know-how for distillation in their to attempts to desalinate seawater. That may not have been all they were using it for. There are references to "strong wine" but whether this something akin to modern grappa (spirit made from distilled grapes) or just a high alcohol wine is unclear. And yet the even the Biblical book of Proverbs talks about wine causing people to hallucinate. That's a tall order for wine.

Do we assume that the ancients made it differently and therefore the stuff had hallucinogenic properties? Maybe. Was "strong wine" in fact grappa? Also maybe, even probably. The answer may be a little simpler than that. Alcohol is a psychoactive drug, and like most psychoactives, it'll do pretty much whatever it is you *think* that it will do. To be clear, not whatever you want it to do – whatever you think that it will do. If you truly believe that grappa is a hallucinogenic, then it probably will be. In fact, if we really get into the nitty-gritty of it, you don't even have to be ingesting alcohol at all to get drunk. Sometimes it is enough to simply believe that you are drinking to tie one on.

One summer in college, my older brother Larry (he of Murffbrau fame) worked at a faux grass-hut beach bar in Florida. In walked a kid with an obviously fake ID. Admittedly, this was a place that took state drinking laws as more a suggestion than a commandment. Still, the kid looked like a kid and his ID was so bad that Larry thought he'd get in trouble for serving him. Instead of refusing service, he took the kid's money and served him virgin daiquiris all afternoon. Somewhere at the tail end of virgin daiquiri number two, the kid got louder, a little more boisterous. After three, he started slurring his words. By number four his friends had to take the legless boy back to the hotel because he was making such a colossal ass of himself.

Proving, if nothing else, that some of what booze does to us happens simply because that's what we expect to happen.

Any culture that produces philosophers by the sackful the way that ancient Greece did, is bound to have the odd swing-and-miss. It's not like Chrysippus was a bad philosopher, either. He was actually well regarded in his day as a prolific writer of Stoic philosophy.

Stoicism, if you're wondering is all about accepting the moment as it presents itself, free from the desire for pleasure or the fear of pain. He also believed in deterministic logic in which events were mapped out by preexisting causes. As a young man, Chrysippus had lost his inheritance when it was seized for the king's treasury. That is the sort of thing that make a fellow stoic, so maybe he was onto something.

In a very Greek way, he died at the age of 73 during the games of the 143rd Olympiad in 208-204 BC. It wasn't terribly stoic, though. There are two accounts of his demise, one where he drinks some uncut wine, gets dizzy and dies tragically, but with some shred of dignity.*

The other account is that he saw a donkey eating low-hanging figs off a tree. Chrysippus tells someone to give the donkey some uncut wine to wash the figs down. Four-legged zaniness ensued and Chrysippus the Stoic died of laughter … watching a drunk donkey.

* Which is why you cut your wine at the symposium!

OLD HABITS DIE HARD

It seems strange that modern Greece doesn't have much of a reputation for wine as they were the first ones to go wide with the vino. Old habits die hard and tastes change a lot faster than traditional methods. France still makes some of the best wines in the world, but in a world of extreme flavors, some French wines can be too subtle for their own good. Not for me, but I'm always amazed the number of people who seem to be gunning for the alcoholic grape punch.

If you want to take a peak into a wine fortified with the traditional resin, try a Greek white wine called *retsina*. If you scrub around, you can still find it. I went to my local wine shop – Buster's – known for selecting it's own bourbon barrels and a wine selection running from Tuesday night *vin ordinaire* to an appointment-only wine cellar. I found a bottle of Kourtakis Retsina – which did not require an appointment and cost about $10. That gave me pause – I'm a value wine guy and I've had few of $10 bottles that have been pretty good. The price wasn't the sin, it was that there was no higher end *retsina* options at all. I think Buster's carries just enough for the large Greek Orthodox church about a mile up the road.

It's an interesting wine – more tart than sweet, bright, not terribly nuanced and, yes, glimmered with that hint of sap. It wasn't really awful in a when in Rome (or Athens) sort of way. It was just a hint of resin, not what the boys at the symposium were tossing back. Whats wrong with sap anyway? People across North America cover their pancakes in maple sap. In your wine though? Fair point.

Mrs. M and I paired it with something called *garides souvlakia* – a skewered shrimp dish. She promptly switched to a Pinot Grigio, whatever that tells you. Being a skin-flint, I persevered. I may have been right about the Orthodox church connection because it tasted, well, sacramental. To say that the finish was long wasn't the half of it. The taste just sort of clung to the tongue and I had a mild headache in the morning.

It would have tasted better with pork rinds.

Richard Murff

CRAPULUS SUM

It took some time for the Dionysus' popularity to spread among Romans. In the late republic, when building towards empire, Roman life was serious, single-minded and decidedly lacking in orgies. Still, the one Latin phrase that I learned at Christian Brothers High School that stuck with me all these years of not using Latin was *Crapulus Sum* – I'm wasted.

At 17, I thought I was being clever but the fact is that while the Roman republic went in for all that "free citizen" business, in a lot of ways the hyper-competitive Romans were more like the Spartans that the Athenians. Drunkenness was considered unmanly. In Rome, wine was not consumed on the near constant basis as in other urban cultures as the Romans had been sober enough to invent aqueducts to bring fresh water in from the countryside.* In fact, Romans of the earlier republic were such wet-sandwiches that one Roman proverb runs "Three things are bad: Night, women and wine." Talk about a bunch of fun-haters.

---

* Albeit in lead pipes. They never figured that one out.

Then, somewhere in that grey area of the late republic and early empire, Rome got so rich that the old ways strained under the pressure and then buckled. As is generally the case, those who inherited the empire were a little more relaxed and decadent that the ones who'd taken the trouble to build it. Morals loosened at about the same rate that social hierarchy tightened and became all-important. Like a later republic *cum* superpower built along its lines, hierarchy was tied almost entirely to economics.

Morals aside, the Romans still found Dionysus's name hard to pronounce in gassed Latin and renamed him Bacchus. According to the Roman historian Titus Livuis the rites were described as "A Hellene of mean condition came, first, into Eutruria, a low in sacrifices..." which is to say, "A low-rent Greek party got popular in Eutruria, where you'd expect these things to happen."

Followers called the festival Bacchanalia. It started out as an annual "girls only" party to honor Bacchus. Whether the Greek *maenads* were real or not, the Roman sorority formed in their honor – they called themselves the *Bacchae* – were certainly of this earth.

In Titus Livius' massive history of the republic he writes that when things were getting out of hand with the Bacchanalias, a free Roman woman named Hispala Fecenia testified as to the orderly nature of the rites *before* the men got involved. The rites were held for three days a year, and by Hispala's account, did nothing more objectionable than have some Margaritas, three-bean salads, and girl talk.

The High Priestess of Bacchus was selected by rotation and when Paculla Minia became priestess, she announced "as if by the direction of the gods" that men were to be initiated. This was probably innocent enough, as the men in question were her sons. Regardless, things went predictably downhill from there. The time of the celebration went from day to night, and jumped from three days a year to five nights a month.

Titus Livius continues his history in a straightforward manner:

> From the time that the rites were thus made common, and men were intermixed with women, and the licentious freedom of the night was added, there was nothing wicked, nothing flagitious, that had not been practiced among them. There were more frequent pollution of men with each other than with women. If any were less patient in submitting to dishonor, or more averse to the commission of vice, they were sacrificed as victims. To think nothing unlawful was the grand maxim of their religion. The men, as if bereft of reason, uttered predictions, with frantic contortions of their bodies; the women, in the habit of Bacchantes, with their hair disheveled, and carrying blazing torches, ran down to the Tiber; where, dipping their torches in the water, they drew them up again with the flame unextinguished, being composed of native sulphur and charcoal. They said that those men were carried off by the gods, whom the machines laid hold of and dragged from their view into secret caves. These were such as refused to take the oath of the society, or to associate in their crimes, or to submit to defilement. This number was exceedingly great now, almost a second state in themselves, and among them were many men and women of noble families.

During the last two years it had been a rule, that no person above the age of twenty should be initiated; for they sought for people of such age as made them more liable to suffer deception and personal abuse.

Livius goes on to opine that it wasn't so much the raucous goings on that freaked the Senate out, but the fact that most were sure their sons and daughters were involved that caused the panic in the statehouse. Whatever the reason, the genie was let out of the bottle. The government got involved and outlawed the party. In pure municipal government tradition, they had to throw in a loophole: You could throw the Bacchanalia if you kept the party to five or fewer. Which, of course, largely defeats the purpose of an unnatural and vaguely homicidal orgy.

With the exemption of the Emperor Augustus – who was always a bit of a prude – the senators were trying to be spoil sports. Having it get out that your son spends five nights a month polluting other boys was as big a political liability. There was more to it at play, however. Romans were very traditional minded: Almost anything was acceptable as long as you could find a "Roman" tradition behind it. While the homosexual rape, bank fraud, embezzlement and murder that went on *was* objectionable, Bacchanalia was really doomed because it was Greek.

What about those Romans who didn't have a father in the senate to annoy? For Romans not born into the lucky sperm club, the only way to get ahead was to attach yourself to some rich guy (who knew full well what you owed him) as a sort of sycophant-in-waiting. It was called a Patron/Client arrangement and Roman civic society was built around it. The central piece of this foolishness was the *convivium* which was something like symposium, but horrible. To the modern drinker, the formality of the symposium might be a little strange, but the idea of getting together with friends, have a few drinks and solve the problems of the world is pretty familiar territory. The *convivium* was another kettle of fish altogether.

Imagine a highly scripted Chamber of Commerce meeting, hosted at a private house, where the point was both a networking opportunity as well as pointed social bullying on par with the most deranged high school cafeteria.

The rich Romans who could afford to show-off threw these *convivia* every night. The guest list wasn't particularly elite – you didn't even have to know the host, but could get invited by another guest provided that he was higher up the food chain than you. The seating and the menu, however, were very elitist. In the dining room, the tables were set up in a squared off U shape with guests reclining on sofa along the outside. In the inside of the U shaped arrangement, slaves brought food and wine, cleared away empty plates and refilled cups.

The host and his family* reclined on one side, guests the host might actually like in the middle – the closer to the host being more important. The further you were stuck from the center of gravity was, in effect, a public illustration of your regrettable insignificance. The reason why guests of guests,

---

* Women were there, and I suppose that's some progress.

and even guests of guests of guests were tolerated at the *convivium* was that the host needed someone to publicly humiliate in order to show his honored guest how important and powerful he was. Which was measured by the number of poor slobs he could get to degrade themselves by taking his abuse in return for a for a free meal.

Sounds fun.

Imperial Rome was all about wine, and they were crazy for vintages. During the republic, amphorae was stamped with the year and the name of the annually elected consuls. Like modern wine snobs, Romans would pay up for a vintage. Like modern con-men, Romans vintners saw that if nit-wits with more money than sense were paying a premium for date, just fake the damn date. Roman elite loved red wines – the Sangiovese grape used in so many bold Italian reds comes from the Latin *sanguis Jovis*, "Blood of Jupiter." Connoisseurs almost certainly couldn't tell the vintage as well as they thought, as they cut their wine with hot water.

While the host and his honored buddy were quaffing dubious "100 year old" vintages, a slave was serving you, you mighty nimrod, some ancient equivalent of wine in a can: A second-rate quaff was called "gold wine." Which was made by throwing all the grapes, regardless of color and their skins, together and letting nature take its course.

Stated thusly, the willingness to submit to public humiliation for a slim chance at getting ahead seems very foreign. To me, at any rate. Then I turn on the television and am faced with reality television. Then it seems less… well, it's still weird as hell, just less foreign.

All of which explains how something like the cult of Dionysus got introduced into Italy in the first place. People needed a release from the theater of humiliation that was Roman civic life. It also explains the Roman senate's reaction to things getting really out of control. The senate really didn't like that "state within a state" business Titus had written about. What followed was a McCarthyesque crackdown where cult members were arrested and turned on each other to save their own skins. The powers that be thought the energies and livers of the republic ought to be saved for a more Roman festivity: Saturnalia.

First century accounts of Saturnalia say this, "the most wonderful time, and the worst." Sound familiar? Like Christmas, Saturnalia was only one day, but it managed to take up an entire month in a way that patriotic holidays like the 4th of July and Thanksgiving simply don't. Not that there wasn't a patriotic element to both Saturnalia. To quote an approximate translation of a first century Roman etiquette guide provided by *The Economist* newspaper: "The world's only superpower will never preserve its booming economy without the wild holiday spending of ordinary Romans. In this Consumer-led Golden Age, Saturnalia is no longer an indulgence. It's a civic duty."

In fit of assimilation with their conquerers and new Roman overlords, a minor tribe called the Pindenissitae surrendered to Cicero on Saturnalia to make a gift of themselves. They must have been minor, Cicero wasn't much of a general. Given the man's long-winded and impenetrable Latin, perhaps he confused them into surrender. He sold the 3,000 slaves at auction for 12,000 sesterces.

So the Romans took Saturnalia as seriously as we take Christmas, which is a shame. Still, like us, they went to great lengths to not take things so seriously. In any hyper-competitive republics, we take a lack of seriousness seriously. The Roman attempt to not take things seriously went seriously beyond ours. The head of the Roman gods – Saturn – speaking through his high priest, the Pontifex Maximus, had to tell the Romans to settle down. To use the *The Economist*'s translation further: "During the week the serious is barred; no business allowed. Drinking, noise and games and dice, appointing of kings and feasting of slaves, singing naked, clapping of frenzied hands, an occasional ducking of corked faces in icy water-such of the functions of over which I preside."*

The writer Ambrosius Macrobius wrote of loafing around "most of January." The official closing dates were 17 – 18 December but then as now, most tried to squeeze out a little more holiday - generally about a week. While the courts and schools closed, retail was still on its feet selling those last-minute gifts. Saturnalia was such a production that Romans of any status received so many gifts that most were never even opened, but simply passed on to others. Apparently along with the arch, concrete, and indoor plumbing, the Romans invented re-gifting as well.

Going to the temple on the first day was a must for appearances. The Romans were very pious people, but not in

---

* Singing Naked.

any moral sense of the word. Saturn didn't really care if you polluted boys in March, drank too much, or burned down Carthage when the mood hit. What Saturn *did* care about was that he got his goat or candle wax or whatever sacrifice you could afford. The Romans being Roman, the temple rites concluded with a public banquet (with, we assume assigned seating). Then the celebrants shouted "Io, Saturnalia!" and got funky.

Without a television, the lower classes went to the plays to watch Gauls and other non-citizens get hilariously castrated and eviscerated. Between shows sponsors plugged their wares. At the end the emperor came out and threw wine vouchers into the crowd. Even the Romans, with all their genius, could not make a holiday special worth watching.

Those Romans of quality threw typically lavish dinner parties and played dice like lunatics. A popular game was akin to "truth or dare" meets "strip poker," where an appointed "king" of the game made bets on anything with a pulse and decided who had to tell secrets, lose their clothes and who got a turn on the serving-girl.

According to the Martial, something like a Roman-era Martha Stewart, "People will play for hours."*

For the otherwise practical Romans, Saturnalia was horribly inconvenient. As the Saturn spoke, through his Pontifex Maximus, "When I was king, slavery was not." So there sits the social ambitious Roman man on the make, trying to impress everyone and his in-laws with his

---

* I'll bet.

hospitality, and his slaves are running about, not picking up after themselves, telling you to go to hell and messing up the topiary by screwing in the garden. All this goes a long way to explaining why the rich underwrote that lousy holiday entertainment: They were trying to get the slaves out of the house for a few nights. Still, it was considered bad form to take revenge on the help for their flagrant behavior over the holidays.

Not all the Romans got into the festivities, Seneca wrote that "the whole mob has let itself go in pleasure." Crediting to the Romans the timeless innovation the "When I was kid…" battle-cry of the middle aged man. Like Bacchanalia, all that riotous living generally went no place good. A plot to burn down the senate house was uncovered on Saturnalia. The Emperor Commodus, the useless son of the sensible Emperor Marcus Aurelius, was strangled in his bath on New Year's Eve.*

Eventually, with the onset of Christianity, Saturn was too pagan and got scrapped in favor of a mere winter solstice celebration called Brumalia. Then the Germans sacked Rome and somewhere after that Christmas bought out what was left of Brumalia.

It was that German efficiency. Those people will invade anywhere

---

* He was not, in fact, killed by Russell Crow, as the movie *Gladiator* might have you believe.

Part Two:
Too Much of a Good Thing

Civilization Begins with Distillation

A Vintage To Sniff About

A Drunk New World

CIVILIZATION BEGINS
WITH DISTILLATION

Ole Bill Faulkner, musing over a glass, once said "Civilization begins with distillation." He was also fond of saying "A writer without a bottle of whiskey is like a chicken without a goddam head."

I'm a fan of the man's work, I get it, and have lived most of my life in the same general neighborhood where he spent his. Still, I'm not so sure about that last quip. More generally, I think that Faulkner laid the Southern grotesque thing on a bit thick for his editors and the media in New York. I really do believe that many of the long-held misconceptions of about the South are rooted in the fact that Faulkner got a kick out of shocking the yankee literary set.

So it was a bit of a shock when the writer's name came up in southern Iraq. I was sitting in a well air-conditioned meeting room of a hotel in Nasiriyah, near the Sumerian city of Ur. Situated between the Tigris and the Euphrates rivers, Ur gets a few mentions in the book of Genesis, and is traditionally held as the birthplace of the same Abraham that is claimed in turn by Jews, Christians and Muslims. Civilization here is really, really old.

We've already covered the regrettable state of Sumerian beer, and the evidence that someone, if not Noah, was planting vineyards up in the Transcaucasus to sell to Sumerian and Babylonian mugwumps.

Not wanting to look like a dirty American, I'd re-read *The Epic of Gilgamesh* before heading to Iraq. What I hadn't counted on is that my hosts would draw a line from there, through William Shakespeare and to William Faulkner. This was an impressive feat on the part of my hosts – I'm a bookish guy and can't name one Iraqi writer, including whomever the hell wrote *Gilgamesh*.

Modern Nasiriyah is dry, so we weren't discussing the writer's thoughts on whisky but I was sitting in the cradle of civilization. Faulkner wasn't wrong, I decided, but probably not as right in the way that he thought he was. I didn't dwell on it, they were in a civil war.

Distillation, unlike fermentation, doesn't just happen by accident unless you live in some post-apocalyptic hell-scape where the seas routinely boil. Southern Iraq isn't even *that* bad. The technology behind distillation isn't exactly cutting edge, it *is* a technology. At its simplest, it is boiling a liquid into vapor, capturing said vapor, and turning it back into a liquid. All of which is simple enough. The trick is controlling the process to get it to do what you want.

There is evidence of crude attempts at distillation as far back as 2000 BC – and it seems to have been used to make perfumes and balms in ancient Babylon, just north of Ur. In the fourth century BC, Aristotle wrote that "Seawater can be made potable by distillation*, as well as wine and other liquids can be submitted to the same process."

This was important for the Greeks because, as we've seen, as they had a never ending drinking water issue. The concept was to desalinate sea-water by separating the clean water from the dissolved salt solids by turning it to vapor, moving said vapor to another pot leaving behind the salt solids, where the vapor would cool back into a liquid form without the salt. Given that they were both literate and scientifically-minded, we can assume that the Greeks never cracked this desalination trick on a large, workable scale.

Distillation is great for separating water from solids – but it's also handy for separating two liquids, provided that they have different boiling points. Let's say that after the magic of fermentation you have some nice grape wine. Chemically what you have, among other things, is water – which boils at $212°F$ ($100°C$) – and ethyl alcohol – which boils at $172.6°F$ ($78.1°C$). So, if you can keep the temperature higher than $172.6°$ and lower than $212°$, what will happen is that the ethyl alcohol will turn to steam vapor and the water will not. If the still is sealed, the ethyl vapor will float up as steam does, away from the heat source, down a pipe to a second chamber where, as it cools, it will turn back into a liquid that it mostly ethyl alcohol. Its advanced stage is still pretty simple, but earlier attempts likely involved boiling wine or

---

* The word we use is from the Latin *de stillare* meaning to drip or trickle down

beer and covering the pot with some absorbent cloth or a towel and simply wringing the liquor out of it when it got saturated. Not terribly efficient, and the results are terrible, but it works if your standards are low enough.

By 800 BC the Chinese were using distillation to refine a fermented rice beverage into a precursor to sake. In Egypt Cleopatra the Alchemist* was writing about distillation. Exactly what she wrote is lost, but her writings on the subject are referenced by several contemporary writers.

Across the Sinai Peninsula, the Israelites in the Levant appear to have made something like grappa made from apples called *sheikhar*. The Romans produced a distilled spirit, but its earliest record reference is 100 AD well into the "Real Housewives" stage of the empire.

In one of the oldest surviving text on alchemy, written by Zosimos of Panopolis, mentions a woman known to history as "Maria the Jewess." I suppose that she was, but it seems bad manners to just point it out like that. Maria probably lived in the first century AD in Alexandria, Egypt, and while none of her writings on alchemy survive, like Cleopatra her research is regularly referenced by later alchemists.

Alchemy gets a bad name because its practitioners spent so much time trying to turn lead into gold, but that's not entirely fair. Before anyone knew that the trick was impossible, it was certainly worth looking into the matter. Alchemy, though, was more than parlor tricks, it was an entire field of study, the forerunner of today's scientific age.

—————————————

* Not that Cleopatra.

Of the inventions attributed to Maria's quest to manufacture medicines and perfumes, was the *tribikos*, an early version of alembic still with three arms used to obtain liquids purified through distillation. Also the *kerotakis*, used to heat substances and collect vapors within a tight vacuum, and what is now called a *bain-marie* (named after the lady herself) essentially a double-boiler used to regulate temperature when separating liquids. Which is all that is needed for distillation. And they'd done it by the first or third century

St. Patrick is given credit for bringing the art of distillation to Ireland in the fourth century AD. Maybe, but with no disrespect, St. Patrick is given credit for a lot of things in Ireland: That whole ridding the island of snakes business, for instance. I wasn't there, but the Romans had noted a century earlier that there were no snakes on the island and most scientists now agree that there never were any in post-glacial Ireland. So we need to take some of St. Paddy's CV with a grain of salt. If for no other reason that the implausible snake story was originally credited to another Irish monk, St. Columba, who lived a century later.

Columba is an interesting figure, as he's mentioned in the *Navigotio de Santis Brendan*, an account of St. Brendan's supposed voyage to Iceland and then North America some 500 years before Leif Ericsson and a 1,000 before Columbus.

This business of the Irish discovering America may or may not be blarny. In 1976, Irish historian Tim Severn built a *currah* – as sort of gigantic leather canoe with a sail – from the specifications in the ancient text then sailed the specified route from Ireland, to Iceland and then onward to Canada. Some of the yarns about the journey seem made up, like getting out and building camp on a island that turned out to be a sleeping sea monsters.* Other features of the story seem to be issues of description – the crystal pillars mentioned could easily be icebergs and the descriptions of landfall do seem very much like Newfoundland. None of this proves that St. Brendan actually did reach America, but only that it's plausible. And that the Irish are crazy.

Whether that voyage actually happened or not, Columba did make the shorter journey across the North Sea in 563 AD to Scotland, and supposedly brought with him the art of distillation. And even this is not the man's final dubious clam to fame: Written about a century after his death, there is an account of him doing away with a "water beast" in the River Ness, near Loch Ness.

It's worth noting that the art of distillation was well established at the time the story of water beasts in Ness got written down. You do the math.

Zosimos of Panopolis was an alchemist, but was also a Gnostic Christian writer, and it a largely illiterate world, monks like Zosimos held onto and copied these ancient works. I'm not sure what this says about early monastic life, but what the monks saved included a great deal of thought that the papacy decreed heretical. Locked away and isolated as they were, who could tell what they got up to?

---

* Plausibly a whale, but are they terribly heavy sleepers?

So the monks almost certainly knew about distillation and, well, why not give it a whirl? Understand that if Columba and company were distilling booze in the fourth century, it certainly wasn't anything that we'd call Scotch or Irish whisky. If anything, they were distilling honey-mead or wine for preservation because only a fool or a masochist would have laid up a wine in the fourth century (or 16th, for that matter). What they would have soon learned was that the resulting brandy didn't spoiled as quickly, or for that matter at all.

If the Irish and Scottish monks were, in fact, making brandies, we can assume a couple of things: First is that they did not have the capacity to make a lot of it. Second, they'd have stored the brandy in used wine casks, because that's what they had. Third, like wine, it wasn't bottled but poured out into jugs directly from the barrel for whatever was needed right then. Fourth, almost certainly you discover that it packs a lot more of a wallop than regular wine. And Fifth*, unlike wine, which got increasing foul as more was drawn from the barrel, they would have noted that the brandy got *better* the longer it sat.

Take all these observations together and you have something that is hard to make in large qualities, what is made has a long sit before it's really good, and packs enough of a punch that the monks just might decide really shouldn't be turned loose on the general public. So, like those heretical texts in the basement, they just failed mention the stuff and drank it all themselves.

---

* See what I did there?

I was raised Catholic, and went to 12 years of Roman schooling. So, I mean this with the utmost respect, but this *is* the sort of foolishness you expect of Catholics schoolboys when we spend too much time together. The curve ball in this story of distillation is just who was responsible for making hard liquor go mainstream.

In the Qu'ran, the Prophet Mohammed forbids drinking... eventually. In early Surahs (a surah is like a Biblical verse, only more exotic) paradise is described as having rivers of wine. When good Muslims enter heaven, they are given sealed casks of wine. Surah 16:67 states "And of the products of the palm and the vineyards you take to yourselves therefrom an intoxicant and fair provision."

Understand that, unlike the Bible, the Qu'ran is not a collection of narrative stories and morality tales. It is more a series of pronouncements dictated by Mohammed to his followers, (or according to tradition, by Allah to the faithful *through* Mohammed). It is more like a greatly expanded Ten Commandments than an arc of stories. Still, over the course of the text, there are some warnings against drunkenness, and the foolishness someone is likely to get into while really gassed, but wine on its own is still pretty wholesome: A gift from God. Until ... according to Islamic tradition... a drunken brawl broke out among the prophet's followers during a game of dice.

It is in a much later surrah, post-drunken dice game brawl, where Mohammed says "O ye who believe! Strong drink and games of chance and idols and divining arrows are only an infamy of Satan's handiwork. Leave it aside in order that ye may succeed."

Islamic jurists decided that the last dictate superseded earlier memos on the subject. The whole story has a "This is why we can't have nice things" air about it.

Regardless, the straightforward simplicity of Islam spread – fast. Early Muslim leaders were pretty tolerant of Jews, Christians, and Zorastorians as "People of the Book." For one thing, the Qu'ran commands it.* More practically, the time of Islam's Golden Age coincides with Europe's Dark Ages, so Islamic leaders weren't intimidated by Europeans. They felt sorry for the poor bastards. Until the Crusades, the only white people they ever saw were dumpy refugees from Europe's brutal feudalism. Later Christian retelling to the contrary, Islam's early expansion wasn't so much at the point of a sword as fueled by selective tax breaks and entry into all the good clubs for Muslims.

The rest were what we might call "second class citizens," never really up for the best jobs or neighborhoods, but they were generally left alone. This multi-tiered society meant that the prohibition of booze in Muslim lands was applied *only to Muslims*. Non-believers could drink all they wanted, and did, because the ruling class reckoned that they were going to hell anyway. So booze was around for a thirsty Muslim willing to go slumming in the Jewish or Christian quarters. Although it tamped down on the public spectacle of drunkenness.

During my Murff of Arabia phase, I noted that Islam's proscription against drinking is about as effective as the

---

* Still does, in fact. You know who I'm talking to…

Southern Baptist proscription or any other prohibition that's been tried throughout history. Which is to say, not remotely.

There grew out of the proscription a whole genre of Arabic poetry called the *khamriyat*. The plots, such as they were, generally centered on an illicit night of drunkenness in shadowy non-Mulsim quarters that included booze, food, sodomy as well as the occasional garden variety orgy with just about anyone on hand, whether they wanted to be involved or not. The end result of these poems can be a bit rapey. The contemporary appeal seems to have been something akin to the "anything goes" glamour of the 1920's speakeasy.

There is no evidence that Jabir ibn-Haygen was into any of the above foolishness when he designed the first truly modern alembic pot-still that made the first effective distillation of what the Arabs called *al-koh'l*. Jabir was an Arab academic who wrote and published on a bewildering variety of topics like alchemy, chemistry, magic, Shi'ite religious philosophy, grammar, medicine and pharmacology. He was smarter than you or me. So much so that it is more likely that "he" was an entire school of academics writing under the same pen name because, you know, branding sells. And at the risk of insulting the reader, even taken separately, these people were still probably smarter than you or me. And as much as it pains me to write, at this distance we just don't know what Jabir's pronouns are: he or they? Or even she: Maria and Cleopatra both lived in Muslim lands. Let's just go with he, shall we?

A century later Mahomed ibn-Zakaryia refined the process of distillation further, again, apparently for perfumes or medicines. The real break-through came in the 11th century when Avicenna invented a coiled pipe that allowed the vapor to cool quicker than the straight cooling pipe.

The East/West technology exchange at the time was huge. For the preceding century, pathetically poor Europeans had been coming to the Near East in waves, then terrifying Europeans in the form of the Crusaders. Then, with the rise of the Ottoman Empire – the Muslim world returned the favor. It's all messy as hell, but historically, this *is* how ideas get swapped.

Christian reformer and legendary doctor, Armaldus de Villanova was born in present day Spain at a time, 1240*, when all the high end-real estate of the Iberian peninsula was in Muslim hands.   He moved to France and gained international fame as a doctor. He is credited with translating several medical texts from their original Arabic – including the above mentioned Avicenna. Villanova was the first European doctor to distill alcohol to use as an antiseptic, and he called it *aqua vitae*: The Water of Life.

Which is all high-minded and wholesome until it the Germans started to produce the stuff for fun, distilling beer into "hot water." In effect the first vodka.

---

* Or there about.

UISGEBEATHA

The Scots would have pronounced *aqua vitae* "ooshkie bayha." Given the long relationship between booze and the divine this "water of life" business isn't a surprise. The modern theologian, however, is not so sure about the boozy magic show. The Christian Brothers and nuns responsible for my education, when forced to explain some of the stranger episodes from the lives of the saints to cynical teenagers, were generally left scratching their heads and saying things like, "Well, boys... historical research in those days was, well *'imprecise.'* [clears throat] But let's not miss the broader point being made here..."

The broader point, as near as I could tell, was that whatever I was doing, I was doing it wrong.

Who knows if St. Patrick brought the art of distillation to Ireland, or if St. Columba brought it over to Scotland a century later before scaring himself senseless on the banks of the River Ness. The broader point, such as it is, is that the locals were some distilling up there, and they'd been doing it for a long time. But it wasn't until the 11th or 12th centuries when the monks started distilling grain.

Again, probably.

Record keeping was a whole lot better then than in 15,000 BC, but it was still pretty "imprecise" by todays' standards. Most records were government tax rolls, and if you could get away without paying your taxes, you stayed off the rolls.

The earliest records of whisky distillation in Ireland date to 1405. The official "birthday" of Scotch whisky is 1495 as evidenced by a birth certificate in the form of an order by King James the IV of Scotland to one Friar John Cor "to make *aqua vitae*, VIII bolls of malt." This is enough malt to make about 1,500 bottles of whisky, so we can assume that this order was not the first one out of the gate.

While made with malted barley, this was still not that hallowed brown water. The friar may have known that to lay the stuff up would improve it, but likely had not stumbled on the innovation of charring the barrels on purpose. So this was likely akin to moonshine, if only a little more mellow. It was not consumed straight but as a base for punches with fruit, honey and spices.

With the Union of the Crowns in 1603, Scotland saw more English soldiers around, and it was they who likely gave the stuff it's modern name when the gallic term was shortened by visiting soldiers to "whoo-skay" and then to "whisky."

The union was really a dynastic affair at a time when nation-states were still the play things of a few wealthy families. Still, the modern world was coming, and it pretty much spelled the end to an independent Scotland.

In 1693 William Paterson, the Scot responsible for the Bank of England, created the Company of Scotland with the intention of making a Scottish colony at the Isthmus of Darien (modern Panama) to manage an overland link connecting the Atlantic and Pacific Oceans. As an investment, the scheme was so popular that it sucked up nearly half the available investment capital in Scotland (by some estimates, 20% of the national currency).

Disease and warlike locals beset the first wave of settlers. So we're clear, the warlike locals in this scenario were the Spanish. The Scottish settlers were so pathetic, the indigenous population took pity and sheltered them. News moved slow back then but money was still being poured into the scheme: Two more waves of settlers arrived to suffer the same fate before Edinburgh realized that the investment was unworkable and the money was gone.

Call it a pyramid scheme or and investment bubble, but it bankrupted the national economy and led to the dissolution of Scottish Parliament. And that laid the ground for the Union Act of 1707 wherein the governments of Scotland and England joined to create Great Britain.

What this has to do with whisky is that a scant eighteen years later, in 1725, London disregarded the treaty that created the Union and slapped a great whacking tax on Scottish malted barley. What the tax did, aside from cause riots, was raise the cost of ale, which was a shame as the introduction of hops really livened the stuff up. Everyone, brewer and distiller alike, was trying to avoid the tax – *plus ça change* – but it's very hard to hide a brewery. Illicit stills, on the other hand are much easier to move around. Just stick it in a barn, behind one of those shaggy cows they've got over there. This is even easier in the Highlands, where government agents wouldn't go if they could help it. This gave whisky that outlaw vibe as a symbol of Scottish resistance.

The new vibe didn't do much fro the lowland whisky producers who had the big commercial distilleries. In fact the Crown's vindictive tax structure pretty much shuttered the industry. In England, the lower classes were all drinking gin thanks to government tinkering. In a last ditch effort to stay solvent, many of the distillers sold their whisky to be re-distilled into gin. And it was these guys who changed how Americans drink when they moved to the New World.

For the ruling elite, their bars were set up a little differently. This was when the upper classes were perfectly fine acting like the upper classes and didn't feel the need to slum it to show they were "just folks." So they kept drinking imported tipples like port, brandy and French wine. Then the Napoleonic Wars happened and suddenly French imports were expensive and – even worse – unfashionable among the Burke's Peerage set.

It was in 1822, that King George IV had a snort of the Glenlivet and Scotch became fashionable in those rarified circles. As it will, Parliament then decided to bring the distillers into the national fold by reducing license fees and taxes so drastically that there wasn't much of an incentive to run the risks of operating outside the law.

Was this an early example of a government increasing revenue by reducing taxes – well, yes, but it wasn't what they were thinking at the time. George IV's father was the loon who'd lost the bulk of the North American Empire over bad tax policy.

A VINTAGE TO SNIFF ABOUT

Wine has, thankfully, improved dramatically since the old days – unfortunately, the wine snob hasn't. As a purveyor of words, I've always thought that the American term "wine snob" missed the mark in describing the creature with which we are dealing. Snobbery implies that all that sniffing at others not being good enough might just be justified. For my money, the Brits have a better term: "wine bore." The term doesn't care one way or the other if the speaker is onto something, they well may be, but it's still tedious as hell to be cornered by one.

For the Romans the snob appeal was stamped right there on the amphorae. As long as the wine bore ignored the near certainty that the vintages were faked – it was right there in the jug to prove your good taste. Just as well because what was on the inside was, even to them, crap. Humans are very resilient creatures in matters both great and small. If crap is all you have, then you can learn to enjoy it. More than that, with a little money and social leverage you can be a complete and insufferable ass about it.

That modern winemaking techniques have delivered a constantly improving product over the last 400 years is something to celebrate: Wine is now a largely stable, complex and nuanced product that does *not* drive people to dose it with tree sap and seawater, or raise vomiting to an art form. Unfortunately, that has only made the modern wine bore *more* boring.

In a republic that prides itself in not being intimidated by class, wine snobbery will still strike a chilling fear down the spinal column of upwardly mobile middle-class Americans. We've always had an inferiority complex when it came to wine though. Thomas Jefferson obsessed over trying to grow old world vine stock or developing a hybrid that would produce something just as good. The first time North American colonies rose up against their European colonial masters wasn't in Concord and Lexington, and it wasn't over taxation without representation either. It was some ten years earlier – in New Orleans – where the citizens rose up and got themselves hanged over at fight for the right to have a nice Bordeaux with dinner. We'll get back to that one later. Over in California, the Spanish Jesuits were growing wine until the Spanish king kicked them out. In the Protestant parts of the country, it was heaps of Norbert grapes from Missouri.

Which to say that we big, loud Americans, rich go-getters convinced that the rest of the planet wants to be us, are nagged that somewhere in the dregs of our psyche that those aloof Europeans are cutting knowing glances at each other that we're doing it wrong. And nowhere does this insecurity float faster to the surface that in a glass of wine.

HILDEBRAD & ARNAUD

Exactly how we got to this state of affairs in dealing with wine is above my pay-grade, but I have some theories. The first is simple enough: market competition. Beer made the transition from old school, chunky booze-porridge into its modern incarnation that we know and love earlier than wine made the crucial leap from sap-laced vinegar that was a cure for not throwing up.

The first documented use of hops in brewing beer dates back to the ninth century, but Hildebrand of Bingen is generally credited it some 300 years later. Hildebrand was a Benedictine nun, eventually abbess, who was a scientist, visionary*, and writer. Regardless of who actually came up with the idea, it was her writings that spread the innovation. And it *was* an innovation.

Despite the great imagery, the idea we have of the medieval alehouse or tavern – raucous with laughter and bands of merrye men – is about as authentic as a Kardashian. In reality, a place where you might stop off for a

---

* Not the Steve Jobs type of visionary, the sort that saw visions. A Joan of Arc with a better beer selection.

beer was the kitchen (or more accurately the place just outside the door) of some poor widow trying to make ends meet after her husband had been clove twain in either a farming accident or quite intentionally by the local baron.

Hildebrand had no idea that hops had an antibacterial effect in the beer, but could see that hops retarded spoilage. The introduction of hops in beer brewing effectively took it from a household product with a shelf life of about a week to something that could be done on a commercial scale, like wine.

This changed everything for both products. Suddenly, brewing was something someone did for a living and might even take professional pride in, as opposed to something squeezed in between laundry, feeding 17 children and sewing your husband's arm back on. As such, simple market competition drove the quality of the commercial product up.

Meanwhile people had been tinkering around with distillation for a millennium *that we know of*. After the eleventh century, distillation really started to really take off throughout Europe. Spirits, largely in the form of whiskies, brandies and "hot water" became all the rage. It's easy to see why. Hops may have extended the shelf life of beer as well as improving its flavor, but spirits never seemed to go bad.

Understand that you were still taking your life in your cups with most urban well-water. The charcoal trick that the Phoenicians had used spread into Africa, but was lost to Europeans after the fall of Rome. The alcohol killed a lot of the bacteria, and well as providing calories, an inherent painkiller, and addressed the grim fact that no one really wanted to face *that* world completely sober. The difference was that now you had options. Wine producers, therefore, had to up their game due to competition. And if that isn't a perennial argument for the free market, I don't know what is.

The Cistercian order was founded in 1098 as a counter-point to the fat, ultra-wealthy monasteries dotting Europe. This stripped-down version of monastic life attracted a certain type of seeker who tended to approach every task with a fanatic zeal; from fasting, prayer, being uncomfortable and tending vineyards to perfection. It was the Cistercians who noted that certain plots and hillsides produced the best quality grapes, and began laying the groundwork for what would become France's current *appellation* system. And it doing so would raise being a pedantic gardener to a matter of one's eternal soul. Reportedly, the wines of Avignon were so good that Pope Urban V refused to move the seat of the Papacy back to Rome. We can assume he had an in with the Cistercians, while the average mortal sinner was stuck drinking vinegar.

In upping its game in the face of spirits and beer, French wine started its long journey from antiquities version of taking twice the recommended dosage of NyQuil to that fantastic, awe-inspiring nectar of the gods, wanking snob-fest (and I mean that in the most positive sense) that we now know and hate.

Richard Murff

WINE SNOB ZERO

Ever since the Romans established a garrisoned port city called Burdigala on the Girandi estuary, the locals have been making wine there. In the beginning, though, Bordeaux wasn't a wine region, but a wine city. The Cistercian monks notwithstanding, at the time a wine was known more by its market or distribution channel rather than its place of origin. Arnaud III de Pontac, a nobleman and president of the regional parliament, owned a wine producing estate that had been in the family for generations (because, of course...). Like all the other wine producers, he sold his product to factors called *négociants*, who did the blending and took the stuff to market.

In the face of competition, Arnaud went full-tilt on the snobbery and decreed that his wine was special and entirely too good to be blended in with the mass-market plonk. In reality, Arnaud was making wine no different from the way his grandfather had done it or anyone else in the region. At the time there were no commercial bottling operations so, like everyone else, he was selling the stuff in huge, wooden casks that weren't anymore airtight than the next guys. Nor did he have an established distribution channel other than the same port as all the other Bordeaux producers.

So how to stop the *négociants* from smiling and nodding during Arnaud's dog and pony show about how special his wine was and then simply blending it anyway? The innovation that he landed on didn't do anything to improve wine. It had nothing to do with production at all but completely changed the way wine was sold and perceived. And it is to his credit* that the wine industry has never stepped away from the device.

In 1660, Arnaud simply doubled the price of his Bordeaux wine. That's it. Now his wine cost so much that the *négociants* didn't want to blend it with the more ordinary plonk they also sold.

As for the consumers, they just assumed what they always do when it comes to non-essential products: If a product costs twice as much, then people must be willing to pay the premium. If that's true, then there must be a good reason for the premium. Ergo, Arnaud's Bordeaux, sold under the name Haut-Brion (a name that meant nothing to anyone not from the region) must be better than the usual stuff out there. It really is amazing what we can convince ourselves when both rich and insecure.

We have no idea what a jugful of Haut-Brion tasted like. If it was any better is a little hard to decipher, but we know from contemporary accounts that it was perceived as something apart from the ordinary. And in a trick of snobby self-fulfilling prophecy, it was different. For one thing it was the only wine on the market that wasn't blended. It became something people who could afford it (most couldn't) were

---

* And I mean that in the sense that I wish I could get away with it.

willing to pay for. In the words of no less than the author Samuel Pepys, who had some at the Royal Oak Tavern in London (in fact owned by Arnaud): "Drank a sort of French wine called Ho-Bryan, that hath a good and most particular taste that I ever met with."

And like that, the wine critic was borne out of the otherwise talented writer.

It can't all be hype though, can it? There has to be some real, even scientifically observable innovation that took wine from there to here. There were plenty, in fact. And like most innovations, none of them were moonshots, but a series of improvements along the way that eventually caused the whole thing to hit a tipping point.

Glass blowing stretches back into antiquity but, like distillation, it wasn't all that useful at first. Early glass was pretty, delicate and useless for durable storage. Wine on the Mediterranean was shipped in clay amphorae, but overland, the Romans found that wooden barrels to be easier to handle (although much worse for the product inside). In either case, both started spoiling once the vessel opened and the wine exposed to air.

In 1615, Sir Robert Mansell, a retired vice-admiral, applied for a royal patent on a glassworks that was fired by coal rather than wood. Unlike the delicate, crystal clear glass from Italy, the intense heat of his glassworks rendered bottles that were green or brown and much stronger.

The next generation of glass came from an eccentric ex-political prisoner (he was Catholic and a Royalist, as well as just a little weird), called Sir Kellum Digby, who added a blower to the furnace to increase the heat even further. Soon, glassworks producing the "English Bottle" were popping up everywhere, and by the 1680's wine was being stored in bottles. The producers still sold the stuff to the *négociants* in wooden casks, but marketers and retailers quickly figured out that if you bottled the whole cask at once into glass bottles tightly corked, the entire consignment stayed fresh longer. For years in stored correctly. Suddenly wine had a shelf life, or in winespeak, a vintage worth sniffing about.

The benefits were *not* egalitarian. Bottled wine was expensive, and soon all the estates were charging out the *derriere*. Beer was for the middle and lower classes, wine was for the refined upper crust. And we're still wrestling with that one.

By the mid-eighteenth century scientists were studying the actually chemical process of wine and next the century took baby steps towards Louis Pasteur's growing-breaking work that explained not only the *how* but – Hip Hip! – the *why* of fermentation. A great number of his assumptions have since been corrected and even disproven, but he was the one who first zeroed in on the yeasts, as well as the fact that too much air prompted the bacteria that made it all go off.

And that was the key to everything.

Coitus Interuptus

Remember gentlemen, it's not just France we are fighting for, it's Champagne!" A young Winston Churchill described the mission of his men in the First World War. Noël Coward drank it for breakfast, or what the rest of employed humanity calls "lunch." Big Papa Hemingway drank it at bullfights. We mortals generally toss it back the night we get saddled with our in-laws and leave it at that.

Despite this, the story behind champagne isn't all that romantic or, for that matter, French. After World War II, French authorities began to investigate people selling pre-war Champagne. The authorities were sure that the 30 era vintages were faked for the simple reason that during the war the invading Germans had literally drunk up *all* the Champagne in France. All of it. If you wanted those vintages of the bubbly, you'd have to find it in a cellar somewhere in Britain – who likely sucked down the last of their stash on V-E Day. Which is not the first time that the English had a huge impact on what is essentially a French product.

France's Champagne region is in the north of the country, where it's colder and wetter than its other famed wine regions. So cold in fact, that the juice generally stops fermentation (those yeasts sucking up sugar and spewing out alcohol), and then picks it back up in the spring thaw. As a result, there was often unreleased carbon dioxide when it was shipped in wooden casks. Wood isn't airtight so it dissipated slowly, and then all at once when the bung was pulled. Then the wine would settle down into what was supposed to be: Tart and still. If it was still suffering from gas by the time it got to Paris, that was considered a flaw.

It's true that the iconic Benedictine monk, Dom Pierre Pérignon, spent his days trying to both perfect and promote champagne. He may have even made that famous "I am drinking stars!" quip. If so he didn't mean it the way we think he did. Dom Pérignon spent his days trying to keep bubbles *out* of champagne. When he died, in 1715, though, his baby was already on a different track.

The drink we now refer to as sparkling wine can't be stored for too long in air permeable casks. So, for the next stage in the development, we have to circle back to that eccentric Englishman and former political prisoner, Sir Kellum Digby and his strong, globular bottles with the long necks and tightly secured corks. The wine and the new technology were introduced to each other by another fellow who'd gotten crosswise with powers that be the same year as Arnaud III's genius price hike in Bordeaux.

The Marquess de St. Evremond, was a court hanger-on and charming gadabout in Paris. As charming gadabouts will, he'd written satirical letter which infuriated a Cardinal Mazarin, one of King Louis XIV's more powerful and humorless ministers. It being a gentler age (for aristocrats, at any rate) St. Evremond was able to take all his casks of

Champagne wine with him into exile. On landing in England, he happened to bottle the wine before the second fermentation kicked in. He was trying to prevent spoilage, not invent anything new. Then he presented it to the English court like any good guest does when someone offers shelter. The glass bottles were much less air permeable that wooden casks, so the CO_2 stayed in the wine until the corks were pulled or, for the first time in wine history, popped. The English court went wild for the stuff.

Ever the *bon vivant*, St. Evremond ordered more champagne and bottled it in those sturdy English bottles, so the bubbles came out in the glass and tickled the ladies noses in that groovy way it still does. It's hard to argue that St. Evremond did it for science, or even industry. This scheme has sex and money written all over it.

Let's face it, it still does.

Richard Murff

A DRUNK NEW WORLD

In pre-Columbian Latin America tossed back
something called *pulque;* an oily, milky white drink
that would have packed about the same punch as
contemporary beer but was made out of the agave plant.
You might be tempted to say this was an early version of
tequila, but *pulque* was more like a cloudy aloe cider.

It doesn't seem like anything you'd want to drink, but
drink it they did because the Aztecs were always passing new
edicts and laws banning the stuff. *Pulque* was illegal for
everyone but the elderly and religious rites, so almost no one
drank it. If we apply a little historical deduction, we can also
assume that everyone was drinking it.

There was a recurring, almost universal, fear in the
European exploration of the New World of running out of
booze. Like the fellows up in Apollo 13 had about running
out of air. The Spaniards didn't set out to invent tequila,
what happened was that they'd run out of the rum they'd
brought and didn't have any sugar cane handy. Tequila is just
an attempt the make rum with local ingredients. They saw
the locals drinking hooch made from agave and applied their
methods.

And their methods were pretty clever. Europeans were a technologically advanced people, they knew about trade winds and that the earth was round and not the center of the universe. They were turning the first tumblers to unlock the human genome and about to unleash representative governments across the world. Yet somehow, through all this advanced learning it didn't occur to them not to take a dump in their drinking water.

There is no evidence that the indigenous north Americans had any sort of alcoholic beverages or drinking culture. That having been said, they seem to have know which mushrooms were, say, far-out and which were right-on.

W e know that by 1587, settlers in the Virginia colony were attempting to malt corn to brew ale in the absence of barley. America's inferiority complex with beer goes a long way back because 1607 was the year the first shipment of beer arrived in the colony from England.

America, however, would find its drinking legs. In 1612, Brewers Hans Christianssan and Adrian Block established the first known American brewery on the south end of Manhattan. The club scene must have been hopping because it is in this same brewery, it is claimed, where Jean Vigne, the first white American male was born.* And it is not without significance that he not only born in a brewery but spent his

---

* He's predated by Virginia Dare, born in 1587, but no one knows what became of her. Both were predated by the Snorri, the son of Gudrid, the sister-in-law of Lief Ericsson.

entire life swimming in the stuff. He became the first colonial born brewer.

In 1620, fearing that the new continent might develop a sense of humor, a group of political refugees left Europe behind to find a new life. They landed in a spot they called Plymouth Rock, after a town in England they hated so bad they risked their lives to leave. The place was cold, craggy and rocky and suited the pilgrims to a tee.*

In *History of Plymouth Plantation*, the first governor of the colony, William Bradford, sets out the story of this early settlement in American history and folklore. As a history, it's hard to read because Bradford can't stop assigning everything to Providence. Even when one of the Mayflower crew whom Bradford doesn't like comes down with "a grievous disease, of which he died in a desperate manner" and is thrown overboard, he explains that "it pleased God."

Providence, according to Bradford, led the Puritans to a place suitable for settlement. A more practical legend has it that they stopped in Plymouth because they were running out of beer. Bradford doesn't cite this in *History*, but given what happened next, there may be something to the story. The Puritans reckoned Plymouth was suitable because they saw that some "savages" had been growing corn there. This was short-sighted because just a little further on, three rivers empty into the harbor at Boston. For a colony dependent on fur trading, those routes inland would be crucial.

---

* The term "pilgrim" means a religious seeker, and has been applied to the gang on Plymouth Rock because it sounds better than what they called themselves: Separatists. A term now used to describe nut-jobs.

God's mysterious ways aside, the pilgrims came to America to build their "city on a hill." Noble enough, but that sort of labor will really work up a thirst. The Puritans were a radical bunch when it came to things like religion, the soul, and their relationship with their maker, but they weren't radicals when it came to science. It never occurred to them that the New World water wasn't as awful and the water they'd left behind for the sinners.

The first "calamity" they faced was not a brutal New England winter, but the crew of the Mayflower forcing them off the ship before the passengers drank all the beer for the return trip. They thought that being left in the inhospitable shores without a keg or two of the good stuff would be a death sentence. And given the high-strung nature of their leadership, they were probably right. The crew of the Mayflower apparently thought this too, it just didn't bother them so much.

Fortunately, according to Bradford, God smote the crew, killing off half off them. Captain Jones took this as a divine signal that the Almighty wanted his pilgrims to have a few barrels of beer, and acquiesced.

In retrospect, all this fretting was a little silly as there was a perfectly good, state of the art brewery down in Manhattan, churning out beer and children. But they were Dutch and to a first-rate Puritan, that crew was just a little *too* liberal.

All the beer swilling aside, the Puritans were not party animals. Like the small villages of Europe, there was a lot of social pressure to ensure that drinking didn't get anyone sideways. If you over-indulged, it wasn't just a hangover that awaited you, but possible jail time and social ostracism.

Like those glorified apes in Chapter One, being a social outcast in colonial America was not a matter of smoking too much and annoying your parents. Like drinking, it was a matter of life and death. Brooding loners weren't long for this world.

Still, however, there were places they could go.

AMERICA'S FIRST
LOUSY NEIGHBORHOOD

His name was Thomas Morton, and he was most definitely *not* was not a brooding loner. He liked company – female company – and heaps of it. He was born in 1575 into Devonshire gentry, and moved to London to be a lawyer. There he behaved like most ambitious men from the country when they find themselves in the city with disposable income: gambling, drinking, and semi-comical nudity.

He went to work for one Fernando Gorges, who had interests in New England. Not that Morton had any intention of going to America; he was going to get married.* As it was, a Puritan relation derailed his wedding plans. This, too, was shortsighted. All things considered, the Puritans should have opted to sacrifice one of their own to keep Morton in England.

So to America he went in 1622, returning the next year to say that the Puritans had *not* developed a sense of humor in the New World. In 1624 he was off to New England

---

* How much of a dent this was going to put into his gambling/whoring/drinking, we'll never know.

again. This time sailing under a Captain Wolleston, whose first name seems to be lost in the mists of time along with the identity of the 30 indentured servants they were hauling. Once in America, they talked the Algonquin Indians out of a strip of land to set up a trading post known as Mount Wollestan.* Their niche was selling guns and liquor to the locals. This was illegal, but as it was a Crown-sponsored venture no one took much notice. Except the Puritans, who decided that roving bands of drunk, well-armed Algonquins was definitely not as pleasing to God as snuffing sailors when they get stingy with the beer.

The two neighborhoods would have probably peacefully coexisted, each sneering at the other, had not Wolleston started selling indentured servants to planters in Virginia colony. It's unclear whether Morton took exception to being left out of the scheme, or just thought that slavery was no way to treat a white man, but he encouraged the rest of the inventory to revolt and Wolleston fled to Virginia.

Without the stabilizing influence of a hated commanding officer, Morton became the first in a long line of imperial Englishmen to go native. Imagine Joseph Conrad's *Heart of Darkness* with Kurtz as quick with a drink and good with the ladies. The colony was re-christened Merry Mount, and the indentured servants declared freemen. Some attempt at integration with the local Algonquins was made, but this didn't amount to much more than playing kissy-face with the local girls.

---

* Now Quincy, Massachusetts.

History, especially history involving religious movements, is subject to revision and too much emotion to be taken at face-value. Some have cast Thomas Morton as a pioneer in eco-friendly multi-cultural deism. This is a bit strong. It's also largely based on some bad puns in Bradford's *History*. Morton was from the High Anglican Church, but can't be accused of taking it seriously. His main offense seems to be getting drunk with the locals and erecting a maypole, an old Devon tradition dating to pagan times, which held about as much of its original religious significance as the Mardi Gras does now.

In Chapter XIV Of The Revels Of New Canaan, Morton describes the offending:

> The inhabitants of Merrymount ... did devise amongst themselves to have ... Revels, and merriment after the old English custom ... & therefore brewed a barrel of excellent beer, & provided a case of bottles to be spent, with other good cheer, for all comers of that day. And upon Mayday they brought the Maypole to the place appointed, with drums, guns, pistols, and other fitting instruments, for that purpose; and there erected it with the help of Savages, that came thither of purpose to see the manner of our Revels. A goodly pine tree of 80 foot long, was reared up, with a pair of buckshorns nailed on, somewhat near unto the top of it; where it stood as a fair sea mark for directions, how to find out the way to mine Host of Ma-re Mount.

Morton's Christianity was attacked, although there probably wasn't much to attack. The Puritans saw drunken fornication with native women as giving ground to pagan orgies that they'd taken the good time and trouble to leave in the old country. In Plymouth, the High Anglican church was only few Hail Marys better than the Roman Catholics. Which, the Puritans reckoned, was another religion best left to the Old World. While it's much handier to tell school children that the Puritans came to America seeking religious tolerance, it's completely wrong. They'd found that in Holland, where they were pretty mellow about a lot of things. The Puritans were seeking a nice place to exercise their own religious intolerance.

In the New World, they faced another problem of a more secular nature, one familiar to every salesman who was ever gone drinking with a customer. Both Merry Mount and Plymouth were primarily trading operations, which meant developing local business relationships. Regardless of race or culture, people can generally tell when another person holds them in contempt. For that reason, the Algonquins just liked the Morton and Company better. They were friendlier, drinks were better, and the locals were invited to the party. Merry Mount became the fastest growing colony in New England and was stealing a huge chunk of the fur trade that Plymouth was looking to monopolize.*

In 1628, on the second annual May Day "Revels of New Canaan", the girl-shy Miles Standish raised an army of

---

* William Bradford never speculates about God's opinion on anti-trust laws.

about nine men to go set things right. Morton called Standish "Captain Shrimpe," because he was short, the Algonquins called him Little-Pot-That-Soon-Boils-Over, because of his temper. Priscilla Mullins, with whom he was smitten, called him unlucky in love and married his best friend. All of which would account for all the pent up anger.

The ensuing battle was not the stuff of Grecian poetry. Merry Mount's "army" was too drunk to hold their guns level and only managed to give the lawn a good aerating. The only recorded non-alcohol related injury was someone listed forward and poking his nose on the point of a drawn sword, resulting in the loss of a little "hot blood." Standish, while no ace with the ladies, could round up booze-hounds and chop down a maypole. Morton was arrested and marooned on the Isle of Shoals off New Hampshire until an English ship would take him home. Or die.

The Algonquins thought the whole thing was pretty funny and brought some food so he wouldn't starve until he got to back to the Motherland. Merry Mount survived another year without Morton, but it was like having the Three Stooges without Curly – fun, but not the same. In Plymouth they recast the place as Mount Dagon because that sounds so much less jovial. And for once Captain Standish got to assign a nickname.

Later that year, Morton returned only to find no one at home. He wandered down to Plymouth, was rearrested and sent back to England. In 1630, the colonial powers that be did what locals governments have been doing to lousy neighborhoods ever since: Raze it to the ground.

England wasn't the best place to be either. James I was dead and his son, Charles was king. Charles dismissed Parliament in 1629 and wouldn't call another for eleven years. He thought Parliament should know its place. He had every legal right to do it, but collecting taxes without Parliament was illegal. So, strapped for cash, Charles couldn't go to war like all the other kings got to do. In 1642, Parliament obliged the king by giving him not one, but two, civil wars. This saved the taxpayer money as they didn't have to ship the army to the Middle East to get to the fighting.

Morton fled to New England again. He landed in Maine and, for some inexplicable reason, returned to Plymouth where he was arrested for being a royalist agitator.* He was sent to Boston where he was imprisoned while "evidence was sought." None was found, so he was released. Then the man moved to Maine, where he knew some planters from Devon and thought it best to get around some familiar faces who'd take the maypole in the spirit it was intended. There he died in 1647.

---

* Thomas Morton was great at a party, but a slow-learner.

That's Not Blood On Your Shirt, It's Bordeaux

T he British and the Dutch imported their drinking habits in the form of beer, and then cider in the American Northeast. The Spanish and the French, however, were winos. Wine is a time consuming affair, trickier to produce than beer. Moreover, the Gulf Coast and the Caribbean are not the places to install vineyards.

Sugar cane, first introduced by Columbus in 1493 grew like wild and, when milled, produced a syrupy run-off molasses, which was great for making rum, which the commoners sucked down. Ladies and gentleman, however, drank wine. And it had to come from Europe.

Almost immediately, the English colonies set about making themselves loyal, but independent, members of an imperial whole in the Northeast. Creating freestanding institutions and electing assemblies from their own lot, the English colonies quickly became self-sufficient and soon enough, a moneymaker for Britain.

Louisiana, not so much. It looked European, or at least tried to. Its governors came from Europe and sailed back when their terms were up. Louisiana was a draw on the

French purse and never really took off the way the Atlantic seaboard did. Most economists would argue that it still hasn't.

The why of Louisiana's failure to launch was not a matter of resources or location. The colony straddled the single most important waterway in North America and was the key to controlling the interior of the continent. To be more precise the colony *was* the interior of the continent. It wasn't a late start, either; the Spanish had sailed along Louisiana's gulf coast in 1520 and found the Mississippi River overland in 1542. Spanish imperial aims were shortsighted, however, and settling the drainpipe of the New World wasn't on the agenda. They were just snooping about in case Aztec gold ran out before they could outspend England in a naval arms race.

It wasn't until 1682 that René Robert Cavelier came down the Mississippi to its mouth and claimed the whole place for Louis XIV. Understand that the place in question were all the swamps and bayous, the Mississippi River up to the Great Lakes, the prairies and great plains of the mid-west and west up to the point where they'd start pissing off the Spanish again in California. Thomas Jefferson's purchase of Louisiana for $15 million dollars has been described as the greatest real estate deal in history, but considering the French just found the place lying on the ground, who knows?*

In 1699, the first permanent settlement in the area was made in Mobile. It was not a profitable colony. There was nothing to eat but oysters so the colonists invented Mardi Gras to pass the time before they died of malaria, yellow fever, starvation, boredom, or in some bloody Natchez Indian religious ceremony.

The Caribbean and the Gulf Coast areas were not then paradise holiday destinations, but a death sentences. No one went there to start a new life unless they had been forced. The idea was to go to the islands, make a fortune while not getting killed by some dread disease or a slave revolt, remove yourself – fortune in tact – back to the Old World. There you bought a title and pretended your money was much older than it actually was. The end result was that the Latin colonies had neither homegrown leaders nor institutions with the administrative experience.

Enter John Law, a Scotsman. He invented the first real estate bubble in American history when he decided that Louisiana, with little to no local administrative oversight, was a good a place as any for a pyramid scheme. Law was a convicted murderer in Scotland, but age and the Parisian café culture had mellowed him. Given the success the

---

* The French were wily this way. When Napoleon sold the colony to the US, he threw in the West Florida to sweeten the deal. Florida belonged to the Spanish. Which is like having a yard sale and hocking your neighbor's couch. Jefferson thought a deal was a deal, and established the long-standing American policy of ignoring all Spanish claims to anything.

English were having in New England, the original investors in Law's Mississippi Company thought they were onto something big. Law soon discovered two things: a) that the colony wasn't profitable but... b) if he paid out unbelievable returns, no one would bother to check on a). The onion, then and now, was that to keep paying those skepticism-crushing dividends, without turning a profit, you need a constant flow of new investors. When you are paying fantastic returns, that's fairly easy.

Until it's not.*

The French had grand visions of the place even if no one was actually there. The colony itself was a sinkhole, but investment capital was pouring in regardless, and places like New Orleans were being built. More money, it seems, than people because it took thirty years after *Neuvelle Orleans* was laid out to actually fill up with colonists.

What few colonists there were came from cleaning out the jails in France. When they needed wives, the women's prisons were emptied. On paper this should have done the trick, but contemporary accounts have most of the "wives" taking one look at the place (or their prospective husbands) and disappearing into the wilderness with Natchez women. No one bothered to go after the runaways because the Natchez had a religion so bloody they made the Aztecs look like Quakers. The French Crown just sent over more prostitutes.

---

* The Scots, it would seem, have an unsung genius for real estate pyramid schemes.

It's a shame that the Natchez had no written language. The record of a small, homogenous and isolated community suddenly swamped with bone-white and terrified whores who smelled like sweating cheese and speaking an entirely alien language would surely be a potboiler.

It was a M. Pierre Druex who bought one of the first plots of private land in New Orleans, near what is now the Vieux Carré. His plantation was named *La Brasserie* or The Brewery because before he planted crop one he built a malt liquor plant. There was a sound reason for this. Ex-cons, of any nation or age, are still ex-cons. They tend to be thirsty.

While the convicts drank whatever M. Dreux brewed up, the paper-thin upper crust in Louisiana was drinking wine. So deeply rooted in their French souls were the colonists that they refused to believe it when news trickled in from the motherland that they were no longer, strictly speaking, French.

France ceded the colony to Spain in 1762 in a secret treaty and was glad to be rid of the place. Spain had just entered the Seven Years War (known in the Americas as the French-Indian War) on the side of France and, like France, was about to lose. You know how the French are; they just weren't going to give it up to the English.

Both Spain and France thought so little of Louisiana that neither bothered to change out colonial administrations for nearly a year after the swap. This served everyone's purpose. For their part, Louisianans didn't think much of "yankee" America. The settlers were proudly French and looked with

Gallic distain on the rest of the continent. The problem after the swap was that they never really became Spanish either.

When Don Antonio de Ulloa, the first Spanish governor, finally arrived he found a poorly run, corrupt city firmly in the hands of organized crime and smugglers. Much the same as it is today. In an attempt to make a profitable colony where the French had failed,* Don Ulloa decided to stamp out smuggling by banning trade with France. This was irksome, but it was assumed that French wine, that staple of the New Orleans diet in proper circles, would be exempt. The Spanish governor was thorough and said *no más* to French wine.

Thus, in 1768, started a rather bloodless revolt involving throngs of well-heeled rioters crowding into the city square and demanding the head of Don Ulloa and a nice glass of Bordeaux. It was also the first attempt in American history to throw off the shackles of a European power and establish an American Republic. Not over taxation without representation, or religious freedom, this revolution's aims were more practical: The right to have a decent glass of wine with your étouffée.

A year later Alexander O'Reilly, an Irishman in the service of Spain, arrived with 2,000 Spanish and Irish troops (imagine the drinking games in that crowd) and promptly did nothing but stand around.

This was enough for the architects of the revolution to start grumbling about how they didn't have anything against

---

* In defense of the French, they didn't try very hard, and they had Bernie Madoff's godfather running the books.

the Spanish Crown *per say*, just Spanish wine. What's more, the rebels added, they didn't actually kill anyone, just indulged in a little seditious fuzziness.

Don O'Reilly said all was fine, and invited the conspirators to dinner to bury the hatchet. There he had them arrested and five of them shot. For this he's called Bloody O'Reilly. A great deal of historical research is placing events in historical perspective. Having a revolution, then a crushing counter-revolution with only five fatalities, at a dinner party no less, is hardly worthy of being called "Bloody."

The French tend to get emotional when they drink.

THE DRINKING REPUBLIC

Meanwhile, back in New England, the revolutionary undercurrents were slowly heating up with more steel in their spine. Whether they remained part of the British Empire or carried on alone as a republic, America was home. The colonies weren't an exile or a temporary post where you hedged a death sentence against a posh retirement and a title for the kids. For English colonists, America was the future.

The tide of American opinion has always been something that can go from lukewarm to boiling over almost instantly. Until the eleventh hour, most colonists were happy and proud to be a part of the empire that was emerging as the greatest since the fall of Rome. As such, the drinking habits of colonial America mirrored closely that of Europe. Laborers were paid in liquor rations because it helped the day pass in a convivial mood.

Yet drunkenness was relatively rare. That the New England colonies hadn't been entirely stocked with anti-social felons like Louisiana or Australia must have something to do with it. In their first hours, the colonial towns mirrored their British counter-parts in that most of them were smallish, densely knit communities that were largely self-policing. True, people were fundamentally as lazy and crooked then as we are now, but colonial society was expected to do something about it. The effect was to have everyone up in everyone else's business. Which made going down to the local tavern a little like drinking with your grandmother: It's not that you *can't* drink, but if you get sideways, there'll be no hearing the end of it.

There were laws in place designed to thwart drunkenness and pick up the slack where society dropped short. If a tavern owner extended credit to cover a tab, that debt was unenforceable by law. Making it hard for anyone to get much drunker than the coins in their pocket would allow.

Wave after wave of immigrants washed ashore on the Atlantic seaboard searching for a life much the same as Europe, just a little more open to the little guy. Despite all the efforts to make America into a new, improved Europe, the New World had something working against that goal: Too much space. In cramped, stratified Europe, if you thought the local Duke was jerk, there wasn't a whole hell of a lot you could do about it. If you moved, you'd find yourself on the land of some other baron who was likely the cousin or brother-in-law of the first toff.

In America, if you pissed off the local cheese, you just moved. This generally meant pushing (shoving) the locals out of the way. True, the locals took exception to the maneuver, but given both mind-set and personal hygiene of the typical frontiersman, he was basically a walking bio-weapon. So, the westward expansion into America saw people living further and further apart.

As American colonists got used to a mobility and social freedom unheard of in Europe or even earlier generations of settlers, the strict bonds of the social contract that had existed for centuries were loosened. With fewer people sneering at you, the social reverberations of the occasional bender faded.

There was also the simple fact that, as America came into its own, it began to consume and use its natural resources more and more. As farmers spread westward, they were producing more grain than they could possible eat or sell.* Most of them being Scotch-Irish, they used the grain to make whisky. A single otherwise unsellable bushel of corn could make three gallons of liquor.

Still, the long arm of British colonial policy changed the way we drank. When they blockaded colonial ports to make some imperial point or another, West Indian rum and most of the really good beer and wine got pricey. Homegrown whisky it was.

The colonies famously reacted to British taxation by having enough beer to decide that dressing up as Indians and dumping a consignment of tea into the harbor made perfect sense. The British were furious but by today's standards, America's first act of domestic terrorism seems almost cute.

In the revolt of the its North American colonies, the British were facing stronger stuff that the Spanish Crown. Because the British colonies had homegrown institutions, they didn't face the power vacuums that happen

---

* Saturated market, everyone was a farmer.

after most colonial rebellions. Our founding fathers were already leaders, men of action. They made their own hooch.

Thomas Jefferson was trying to wean America off the Old World's teat by making his own brew and growing his own vineyards. In his heart, Jefferson was a wine enthusiast. Records show that he was replanting Monticello's vineyards almost annually, suggesting that his quest for wine that was "not exactly the same kinds [as in Europe], but doubtless as good" was going nowhere fast. If anyone was going to unlock the secret of bringing European wine to the New World before modern pesticides, it was going to be Jefferson. But sadly, no one was.

He was also a man of science, so much so that his endorsement on a product was sought after. In 1804, Michael Krafft wanted to dedicate his book, *American Distiller*, to the famous man of letters and science to "safeguard against its falling into the general wreck of oblivion."

Jefferson was delighted. His response to the request reveals a very zen approach to life before any white people knew what zen was:

> I see too with great satisfaction every example of bending science to the useful purposes of life. Hitherto chemistry has scarcely deigned to look to the occupations of domestic life. When she shall have made intelligible to the ordinary householder the philosophy of making bread, butter, cheese, soap, beer, cyder, [sic] wine, vinegar etc. these daily comforts will keep us ever mindful of our obligations to her. The art of distilling which you propose to explain, besides it's household uses, is valuable to the

agriculturalist, as it enables him to put his superfluous grain into a form which will bear long transportation to markets to which the raw material could never get.

By early 1812, Jefferson was caught up in the scientific process of making beer. Jefferson did few things halfway. In his search for a fine beer, Jefferson turned his plantation, Monticello, into a one-man prisoner of war camp for a retired English Captain named Joseph Miller.

Miller wasn't a combatant, he'd been on his way to Norfolk with his daughter to claim a Virginia estate left to him by his late half-brother before he'd even known the war had started. During their crossing, the Millers were detoured by a French warship and a British blockade. They eventually got to Norfolk, but six months late. Captain Miller was refused the right to claim the estate because he was English. In all of this foolishness, he and Jefferson met and Jefferson learned Captain Miller had been trained as a brewer in England.

For Captain Miller's own "safety" Jefferson suggested he be interred for the duration of the hostilities at Monticello, where he promptly built a brew house and set Miller to training his slave, Peter Hemmings,* in the art of brewing.

The new brewery was ready in 1814. Jefferson's prisoner of war, Captain Miller, and slave, Peter Hemmings were ready to get started. The alarming moral and tax consequences of such an arrangement aside, the first batch

---

* Peter's mother was the famous Sally Hemmings, his father was...well, it seems pretty obvious.

was a roaring success, and soon his neighbors were coming about, sponging dinner invitations and trying to get the recipe. But neighbors are like that.

Perhaps calling ourselves "civilized" removes us a peg or two from nature. Equally as likely is that enlightened intellectuals throughout history are not as clever as they think they are. It's possible my father was right when he said that anyone who has to tell you how smart he is, likely is a moron. Regardless, it was the humble slave Hemmings who saw that barley was expensive but all of Jefferson's farms and the surrounding continent was lousy with Indian corn. Why not malt corn instead? Because of Peter Hemming's innovation, America may not produce the best beer in the world, but it produces the cheapest. And in certain circles that beats quality every time.

With the war over, Captain Miller left Monticello behind to claim his estate in Norfolk. The place was pretty shabby after years of neglect and to make matters worse the neighbors decided to hate him for being a foreigner. This is pretty thick in a republic that didn't exist 40 years ago. Even thicker considering that Miller had actually been born in Maryland. He went back to Monticello to make more beer.

Jefferson started to write his cronies in Washington to get his buddy re-naturalized and eventually did. Peter Hemmings' fame grew within county, where he went around to the neighbors as a one-man brewing academy.

Mr. Hemmings thoughts on these developments are unrecorded. Because of course they weren't.

Richard Murff

Whiskey Money

As anyone whose has followed the erratic rise of crypto-currencies will have noted, governments are very uneasy with any alternative to the national currency. Even if they have almost no national currency to be defensive about.

The early United States was no exception. At the time, the entire world was, in effect, on the gold standard. Or at any rate, a precious metals standard. That's why the Spanish Crown ruled its South American colonies directly – it wanted to suck up all the bling for itself.

Understand, however, that wealth and money are *not* the same thing. You could make a solid argument that the thing that set America apart was simply that there was no gold or silver to plunder. There was no get-rich-quick scheme for the North American colonies, so they were just left to get on with it. What they did, in the absence of hard currency, gold or "money", was to build wealth.

Spain (or more specifically the Crown) was flooded with gold and silver from South America with money, but not wealth. The end effect was that suddenly a greatly increased money supply was chasing the same goods. Inflation and 'bling' when wild, but it didn't really increase wealth. To use a more modern example: A government can print money willy-nilly, which may put more cash in everyones hands, but inflation tends to erode the value of the cash. Which is exactly what happened to the Spanish Empire, Weimar Germany, and the Carter Administration.

Wealth on the other hand, is created when low-value assets are move up to a higher value. A modern example being a clever boob at Harvard comes up with a new bit of code that allows dateless wonders to rate girls who are *way* out of their league. This is a low-value asset. If, perchance, an even more punchable dork comes along and steals said code to turn it into a platform through which advertisers can track your every online move and most of your thoughts, that would be an example of a higher value asset.

Of course, the example doesn't have to be quite so grand as all of that. You could, for example, simply turn a bushel of unsellable and perishable corn or wheat to a higher value asset – like stable whisky.

What hard currency there was in the United States could be found in the urban areas, but precious little in the countryside. Lacking access to banks, farmers just grew all the grain they were able, sold what they could, ate what they needed, and then turned the rest into whiskey as a durable, transferable store of wealth. Basically, their savings accounts were in whiskey where it would sit until   cash was needed, when it was sold.

The system worked well-enough, but Alexander Hamilton didn't like it. Hamilton was born out of wedlock on the island of Nevis in the British West Indies. He bounced around the Caribbean before being taken in by a wealthy merchant and getting sent to New York for law school. He was not, despite what you might have gleaned from the Broadway musical, a Puerto Rican rapper. As one of the founding fathers, and the one who laid the ground work for the new republic's financial system, he also was the one to raise taxes.

Hamilton thought that raising revenue via a land tax was a bad idea because that was the way the rich and powerful stored their wealth and not being born into it, he didn't want to poke that bear. He was about as elitist as any orphaned bastard made good can be.

Out in the country, however, the bumpkins were storing their wealth in whiskey barrels. Urban elites were drinking a lot of whiskey, so he thought he'd tax the poor peasants making the stuff. Enter the Whiskey Excise Tax to the tune of 60 cents per gallon at a time when whisky would fetch about $1.40 per.

Grating though it was, the issue wasn't exactly the tax itself, but how it had to be paid. In the rural areas, there wasn't much hard currency with which to pay it. The obvious solution was to let the people pay the tax in kind (read: in whisky). Hamilton didn't want the taxes paid in whisky, he wanted cash. So the farmers were forced to liquidate assets (the whisky) at a discount (triggered by the forced sale) in order to pay the taxes on said asset.

Somewhat predictably, this triggered a revolt in 1794 called the Whiskey Rebellion. It spread out through western Pennsylvania and Virginia. The action gets dismissed but at the time, President Washington sent more federal troops against the rebels than were ever massed against the British during the revolution.

And that was that for America's first alternate currency. Well, not entirely. While I was writing this book, I helped a friend of mine who holds office with a small PR matter. Being a politician didn't want to accept a favor, and being a friend, I didn't want to accept cash. He paid me in bourbon.

The strange postscript to George Washington's brutal crushing of the Whiskey Rebellion is that, on his retirement he became one of the biggest whisky producers in the new republic and managed to invent rye whisky in the bargain.

Well, let's back up. Washington didn't invent rye – it wasn't even his idea to become a distiller in his old age. That was the idea of Scot named James Anderson, who'd been born into the fringe of Scotch whisky royalty. By Anderson's day, the royalty had been dethroned by the English tax laws that had practically mothballed the industry. So Anderson was a successful farm manager (but not land owner) in Scotland where, like America, farmer and distiller were never far apart. With the industry crippled from London, Anderson, his wife and seven children sailed for the New World.

Anderson was a man of ambition and tried to get himself hired as the farm manager at George Washington's plantation, Mount Vernon, while the man was still president. He didn't get the job but while working at another plantation wrote again to a retired Washington with a scheme to start a distilling operation. He started on 1 January 1797.

Washington was an aristocrat, but land-rich and cash poor. In short, he was a tightwad. He fussed at Anderson over every expense, including that of barely. And Anderson's solution was even cheaper than Peter Hemmings.

Crop rotation was a well-established farming technique. To prevent the nutrients in the soil from becoming exhausted by over farming, you let a field lay fallow for a season. Unplanted soil erodes easily, so to combat this, you plant covering crop that isn't taxing on the soil, but prevents erosion. A common crop for this was rye, which was thought to be inedible. Anderson looked down and said, "This stuff is cheap and it's all over the place."*

He made 11,000 gallons of rye the first year fetched about $7,500, or about. $150,000 today. Soon Mount Vernon was the largest distiller in the country.

The Marquis de Lafayette - America's borrowed war hero – sampled the rye and reportedly it made a fine impression on the man. Back when the French had something to live for other than wine, they were fairly open to new drinks.

What about that loathsome Whisky Tax Washington had brutally enforced during his presidency? Fortunately for his bottom line, Washington was a notorious and brazen tax cheat. He more or less dared Congress to press the issue but they backed down.

A nation needs its myths.

---

* Or words to that effect.

Part Three:

Wine & Spirits
in the Material World

An Over Dose of Bon Bios

See Thrus

Rum: The Darkness & The Light

Brown Water

Prohibition

AN OVER DOSE OF
BON BIOS

We may talk about that *meet-the-challenge-head-on* spirit of America, but in my experience, the most common reaction to wine snobbery is to avoid the fight and slide back into the warm embrace of whatever social strata you've worked so hard to leave behind.

Never fear though, you've got this. The thing to remember is that winespeak isn't about expertise, it's about what the philosophy professor Harry Frankfurt called "Bullshit." He wasn't being vulgar, but even a Princeton University philosophy professor couldn't come up with a better word for it.

Case and point: One of my favorite movie lines comes from that scene in *Goldfinger* where James Bond, eating with M and Colonel Smithers, the head of the Bank of England, says of his brandy: "I'd say it was a 30 year old fine, indifferently blended... with an overdose of bon bios."

I know that these guys were passing around a snifter of brandy – which according to Bond had been wine 30 years ago, but not anymore. With the proper delivery, though, the facts hardly matter.

Years ago, when I was an investment banker, I applied the "bon bios*" line at a wine tasting because a) I felt out of my depth and b) I'd tasted just enough to think that using a line from *Goldfinger* was a terribly funny thing to do. I dropped the "30 year" bit, and the comment was well-received but unremarkable. Two people were visibly impressed, later asking my opinion on another wine (at that point I couldn't keep a straight face and had to confess). In fact, the only person in the room who actually caught the foolishness I was swirling around wasn't a wine expert at all, but just a die-hard fan of Jimmy Bond.

Like a good movie line, winespeak, for good or ill, is all in the delivery. Think about those stories on *60 Minutes* where the famed art expert can't tell the difference between a six year-old's attempt at finger painting and a Jackson Pollack, or that hot shot Wall Street trader whose ten-year running average is only slightly worse than a chimp with a dart board. If you think an industry can't be based entirely on bullshit, consider that the quants who miss four out of five market corrections still have their careers. Or the generals who spent 20 years and $2 trillion fighting a war in Afghanistan only to leave the place to the same people we toppled in 2001. For that matter, consider any reality TV celebrity or most second term politicians. They may not be good at their jobs, but they are great at *keeping* them, which has a lot more to do

---

* Bon Bois is a cognac growing region known for heavy clay soils, chalk and limestone.

with cunning than expertise. I'm not entirely knocking these epic con-artists, I'm a little jealous: A successful sham takes almost as much smarts as running a successful business.

The trick to winespeak, then, as Stephen Potter wrote back in 1950, is to be "boldly meaningless." French words are best because no one you know actually speaks it – they just know some French terms. Translations are provided here, but they don't really matter. Without the context, your complete ignorance can be hidden. Try the following:

"This merlot has interesting traces of *mer chat!*"(sea cat)

"..the way the *ventre singe* plays on the palette." (stomach monkey)

"the *pipé dés* is overdone..." (loaded dice)

A light just went on, didn't it?

At a tasting, or a party surrounded by people who think they are at a tasting, avoid quoting directly from *Wine Spectator* because chances are all the other wine bores will have read the same issue. You won't get called out, because the only ones who would know are as guilty as you. But they'll know. *Wine Spectator*, to my knowledge, has never mentioned the *mer chat* of any particular vintage. Since wine never really tastes like asparagus or pine tar, discussing its *ventre singe* can't be terribly off base.

I suppose that if you were drinking a German wine, you could say something like: "Why this Riesling has a great *kummerspeck.*" Which, for the record, literally means "grief bacon" and is an actual euphemism over in the Fatherland for the weight you gain from emotional over eating. So not only do your pants not fit, but get to hear a bunch of wisecracks about grief bacon. It has nothing to do with wine, obviously, but I thought you should know the term.

If you want to be a real first-rate ass over your Barolo, learn Piedmontese.

Now that you know the fundamentals, let us apply real world conditions. Remember, though, a wine tasting is *not* the real world – it's a bullshit frappé. Wine drinking on a date, however, is fraught with real and practical danger. Still, sometimes you just have to take the bull by the horns.

The simple rule is: If you're with a first date, don't order the cheapest on the list, she'll pick up the ploy and you don't want to get disqualified for being a skin-flint this early in the game. The most expensive wine will be lost on both of you and look desperate. It's not worth doing until some accurate soundings have been made on the prevailing moral standards. For your sake, hopefully neither is inconveniently high.

Best to follow the Buddha and pick the middle way. Be vague, you don't want to be forced to explain yourself only to find out she actually knows something about wine. And if that happens, just let her order. If she immediately climbs to the top of the price list, know that she's faking it as well. Or she's about to dump you.

Ordering on a whim makes you look adventurous. The goal is not to charm the pants off your date, but as a hedge against having ordered something truly terrible by recasting it as a quirky misadventure from a rom-com. If nothing else you'll have something to talk about.

If you are married, understand that your knowledge of wine isn't going to be what impresses your wife. She already knows that you're a blockhead and has decided to look the other way. Acting like an ass in front of the sommelier isn't going to help. Using your dad voice to terrorize the children into letting the poor lady take a long, uninterrupted bath with whatever "Tuesday Night" chardonnay she keeps in the fridge, however, will make her love you with the passion of a thousand eternities.

ON THE RULES

Y ou might think that all this upstart technology and clear-eyed scientific inquiry would have squashed that quasi-religious reverence for the stuff. And yet the over dose of *bon bios* in wine-speak has gotten worse. For one thing, it's all those damned rules. What makes them so irritating is that even if you did throw them out the window, or never learn them in the first place, you'd probably find yourself circling back that direction anyway.

Generally, you will find that the old rules are the best guides for the simple reason that there was a perfectly good reason people drifted that way in the first place. Those revolting bipedals in Chapter One had to operate on a trial and error basis. I'm all for experimentation, but it also pays to benefit from mankind's accumulated knowledge.

White wine, by and large, tastes better chilled. These days, so do the reds, but only up to a point. That "room temperature" rule of thumb is a throwback to when room temperature was about 62^0. Unless you are at a restaurant that takes wine seriously, or you have one of those wine cellars that looks like a dorm fridge, chances are that you are drinking your red wine too warm by about ten degrees. Try it a little, and just a little, cooler. It's worth the effort. If you live in the South, where the nighttime lows cling stubbornly to the eighties like a Duran Duran fanatic, throw a bottle of pinot noir in the fridge and drink it chilled. I can't see how this would work with a heady Cabernet Sauvignon, but a pinot is pretty light stuff.

On the same page as temperature, is glassware. Here we are in great danger of subdividing this into half a dozen reds and then whites. Don't do this. For one thing it's largely pointless – not entirely, but mostly. The bowl of red wine glasses are more bowl-shaped and tapered at the top to collect the "nose" in the glass. And with more complex reds, this really will lend itself to the overall experience. With whites, being more delicate, this is less important.

One thing that does make a difference with either, and here I'm entirely off-trend, is stemmed glasses. Gripping the bowl allows you to warm a red that is a little cold, but if it's already room temperature, or higher, holding by the bowl will only warm it further. You always want to hold a white wine by the stem for the same reason. When going stemless, hold your glass by the lip.

F ood paring is another area where you'd do well to follow the established suggestions until you know what you like. It does make a difference, but there is no good reason to be an ass about it. The point is to enhance the experience, not prove your ideological purity. Though, for a certain personality type the experienced *is* enhanced by launching into a tedious *"akshullay"* designed, almost singularly, to make present company want to strangle you.

It does occur to me that I watched too many James Bond movies growing up. Here he is again and we haven't even gotten to the martinis. In *From Russia with Love*, Bond is traveling under an assumed name with an eye-watering beauty of a Russian defector posing as his fake wife when he finds himself at dinner with a hitman also traveling under yet another assumed identity of a fake MI6 agent. Cold War zaniness ensues. The hitman exposes himself as both a deranged psychotic and no gentleman (the audience is artfully left to decide which worse) when he orders Dover sole with a red chianti.

I know that we all wish that we were James Bond – and it is awfully nice of him to keep saving the world from its peril *du jour* – but more practically, just because a man orders red chianti with Dover sole doesn't necessarily that he's the murderous minion of the Red Menace. Although it seems that the man has a low opinion of the way the Orient Express prepares its Dover sole.

For one thing, chiantis are made with the Sangiovese grape, a berry so bold that it is impossible to correctly pronounce its name without doing a campy Italian accent. Those Italian reds really come right at you, and your food. Something like Dover sole would be completely lost in the stuff. I wouldn't even put it with a steak – with red meat try a Côtes du Rhone if you're looking for a great pairing.

Italian reds are like that. In Italy's northwestern Piedmont region, Barolo or Barbaresco wines are both dominated by the Nebbiolo grape which is somehow more of a frontal assault that the Sangiovese. Granted, in the last 20 years, Italy has had something of a renaissance in winemaking and its reds, while still bold, are a lot less terrifying than during the Cold War.

What I *would* eat with a Chianti, or a Barolo or Barbaresco is exactly what you'd think goes with it: Italian food with lots of lovely and acidic tomatoes and cheeses that will cut the sensation that you are in a wrestling match with your wine.

Italian whites are a different matter, they are as light and delicate as the reds are bold. Not a crowd for half-measures, that bunch.

All of which are good guidelines, but it's no good being too strict about this sort of thing though. Mrs. M and I throw a St. George's Day dinner every year because I'm a weirdo and she's a good sport. My affinity for St. George stems from stumbling on his legend when I was too young to know that it was just that. As I understood it, the usually exit for Catholic saints was being shot full of arrows, eaten by lions or some other fearsome end. Here was a saint who slayed a dragon and then got the girl.* Well, said the eight-year old Murff, that's the way I want to roll.

The traditional dish served is lamb because, without getting into it, that's just what you serve at a St. George's dinner. While I was in the kitchen attempting to ruin the main course, I had a cocktail I'd discovered that was named for the Saint George – a twist on the martini that involved blue cheese stuffed olives and twist of lime.

---

* In retrospect, I'm sure I made that part up.

Other guest, likely trying to avoid me pressing some mysterious Catholic martini on them, were in the library with champagne & prosecco.

We paired the lamb and rosemary potatoes with a Bordeaux because a) it was a nice dinner and b) after 12 years of Catholic schooling this was a liquid version of lighting a candle to the saints. It was perfect – but I noticed only the fellows were drinking the red. It was warm out, the ladies stuck with bubbly for the duration.

Honestly, it looked pretty refreshing.

And the lesson here is just to drink whatever you damn well please.

SCIENCE V. INSTINCT

Humans are survivors. Science repeatedly tells us that this has more to do with instinct than smarts. When pre-science humans really put their brains to something, we were often wide the mark: Disemboweling virgins so the sun won't eat the earth leaps immediately to mind.

Instinct is another matter. If not perfect, it tends to serve us at least pretty well. We didn't know why we bonded over the sauce (lower inhibitions) we just know that we did. A tightly bonded group was more useful to all involved than a pack of competing scavengers.* Alcohol has long been considered medicinal, even if we didn't know why. And practically, in a world before pain killers, plastic wrap and disinfectants, it was.

A great deal of what instinct told us, science has subsequently proven: That a little booze is good for us. Studies show that moderate consumption of alcohol raises the level of High Density Lipoprotein (HDL) in the body. HDL is known as "the good cholesterol" by those who know

---

* You can see this at play in any of the fine reality programming available featuring a brigade hyper-competitive maniacs competing for some cute young thing's genitals.

these things. To the rest of us, HDL promotes solid cardiovascular health and aids in the fight against dementia. Not only does it help you avoid a heart attack, you are lucid enough to contemplate your good fortune.

Dr. Joseph Kanner, of the Hebrew University of Jerusalem, went a step further to ask why we instinctively pair red wine with red meat in a wonderfully titled paper: "The Stomach as Bioreactor: When Red Meat meets Red Wine." published in the *Journal of Agriculture and Food Chemistry*. Dr. Kanner reports that not only is red wine good for you, it can prevent other things from being bad for you. Red wine, in addition to its HDL boosting properties, is rich in polyphenols: Powerful antioxidants thought to protect the body from cancer and heart disease. Here's the thing, most of the benefits of red wine come not from drinking it alone, but pairing it with food.

Say that you're having a nice steak, that seductive boogieman, and you pair it was a lovely red. When you start to digest the meat, it releases an oxidizing toxin ominously called malondialdehyde (MDL), which is tied to arteriosclerosis, cancer, diabetes and giving the Beef Council nightmares.

Don't worry, enjoy your meal, you'll be fine. Red wine, and all those polyphenols, arriving in the stomach at the same time the MDL is released seems to neutralize the toxins *before* they can get into the bloodstream or guilty conscious. According to the study, the MDL level in the stomach was 50% higher that the control baseline after eating fatty red meat, and some 34% lower than the baseline after red meat and red wine. In full disclosure, the tests were performed on rats – a species not known for carping about *terrior* – so your mileage may vary.

Commenting on the report, although not involved, Dr. James O'Keefe, Chief of Preventive Cardiology at St. Luke's Mid-American Heart Institute said, "This is what I've been telling people for years based on observational data." Then went on to say, "If you have a glass of red wine with your evening meal tonight, your peak blood sugar, if you measured it an hour later, would be about 30% lower than if you hadn't had the wine."

It's this post-meal blood sugar spike that causes the inflammation that contributes to diabetes, dementia, heart disease, arthritis, and a near fatal jump in health statistics. Keep in mind, all the health returns on booze start to diminish rapidly. Overdoing it is likely going to have you staring at the ceiling at 2 am in a sugar rush. But you already knew that.

Again, science has proven our instincts sound:,that red wine and red meat pair well. Like most things that instinctively go together, there is a good reason for it. It's the body making its needs known to those sensible enough to listen.

BUYING WINE

So, whether or not it is proof that God loves us and wants us to be happy begs a really big question that I'm not nearly drunk enough to attempt an answer. The fact still remains that I've never happened across a cache of berries rotting just so or a felled tree o' mead and have never met anyone who has. Meaning that, down here on earth, we are forced to go out and buy the stuff.

Most people with a moderately developed palate for wine will likely be able to tell the difference between a $10 and a $35 bottle of wine. What people with moderately, or even highly developed palettes can't do – and this has been proven repeatedly through blind tasting as well as neurologists studying the pleasure centers in the brain – is consistently tell the difference between a bottle costing say, $35 and $300. There are a few weirdos out there who can pull it off, but not many. I'm not one of them and neither are you.

At the $300 per bottle level, what is triggering your pleasure center isn't so much your palate or anything that happens to be on the inside of the bottle. The joy comes from the perceived value of high-end packaging, snob appeal and joys of virtue signaling. Regardless, neurologists tell us that you *are* getting more pleasure. Delusional, sure, but a win is a win.

Drinking wine *is* a pleasure, and in the pursuit of pleasure, delusion *does* matter. Neuro-science and behavioral phycology studies consistently show that the same wine – but with a higher price tag (or an expensive looking label) are perceived by the brain as better, triggering the pleasure centers more intensely than the perception of plonk.

Similar studies show the same affect with pain killers: Sort chemically identical pills into slick, branded boxes, and others into generic packaging and the "branded" pills will not only be perceived as more effective, they actually *will* be. So raise a glass to the placebo effect and the charming delusion.

The next time that you feel out of water at a wine tasting or one of those wine pairing dinners and everyone is carrying on in aggressive winespeak, know that the odds of all of them actually knowing what they are talking about is about the same as all of them having gone down to the casinos that weekend and hit the jack-pot.

And because I can't leave well-enough alone, I'll suggest that, with a bit of self-awareness and a modicum of mind control, you can enjoy some great wines *without* breaking the bank. At that point, a cavalier relationship with reality can be an advantage.

I'm assuming that if you are just getting to know wine you aren't going to start your journey at $300 price point. Any damn fool can appreciate a $45 dollar bottle of wine. To develop a good, practical palette for the stuff you could do a lot worse than seek out good wines – and they are out there – at the $15 price point.

No less purveyor of old school good taste, intellect and madras shorts than William F. Buckley advised in his 1982 book about yachting across the ocean, *Atlantic High*, not to spend more than an average of $3.50 a bottle. And he was a lifelong and well-regarded oenophile. Adjusted for inflation, that's $9.85 in 2021 dollars. Adjusting still further for the grim market realities of fashionable hype of the 80s and 90s, and that takes us, roughly, to about $15.00.

Understand as well that at this level you will have a greater margin of error. Just accept it as part of the adventure. You don't want to experiment when you've got a houseful of guests and an iconic saint coming to dinner, but otherwise, it can be interesting.

If you know what you like you can find some good wines at a value price. It is important to develop a relationship with someone at a decent liquor store – which admittedly can be tricky as the urge to up-sell is pretty strong these days. I've known the owners of Buster's in Memphis since I was in second grade, although you don't have to start that early. A retailer playing the long game will want to keep your business so really has no reason to do anything but steer you in the right direction if they think that you'll become a regular customer. People remember good customers so they'll have some idea of where you started and the general drift of your tastes. At that point you have yourself an inside expert, a boozy Sherpa if you will.

Of course, said Sherpa will slowly start to guide you in the direction of higher end wines. This is fine, because we've all got anniversaries and birthdays, and, what the hell, we've all got to make a living. What's more, you'll be more confident in your tastes and palette. At this point, you may settle on a $12 bottle, or even ten.

A word of caution here...

Ever since I started writing about booze, I've been told that no wine is too cheap for me to drink. Invariably, this comment is punctuated with theatrically rolling eyeballs. This makes me blue. I generally answered the jab with something along the lines of, "Well, now, you really can't judge a wine by its price." Or, depending how much tasting there is going on, "You probably haven't bought as much sophistication as you think with that over-priced Pinot, you half-wit."

Blame the internet, the global economy firing itself in the midst of a pandemic, or just Charles Shaw of "Two Buck Chuck" fame – but if you really want to cheap-out, you can find wine at bottled water prices, and not the swell reverse-osmosis stuff with electrolytes either. It's a shame because there was a certain profane integrity with the old Night Train and Thunderbird; you knew what they were for. These *neuvo-cheaps*, on the other hand, are masquerading as something else altogether.

Yet I'm a professional, so I felt compelled to delve in and see how low I could go. If we don't learn from our experiences, what good are they? What I've learned is that there is floor to how deep I'll go down the cheap wine rabbit hole. I can't mark the edge exactly, other than to say that it is somewhere *above* $2.99.

Even a cheap bastard like myself had to admit is a comically low price point. I won't mention where I got it because the retailer didn't make the stuff so it isn't their fault. Not entirely. The RICO statutes of this country make it clear that anyone taking part in any part of a crime is guilty for the entire crime. Whatever it is that Burlwood Cellars is churning out is something of a crime.

This wine did to my soul what the villainous Le Chiffre did to James Bond* in that infamous *cane-chair-and-knotted-rope* scene in *Casino Royale*. You know what I mean, right in the pills. According to the label, it was a Pinot Noir, and I doubt they were technically lying. It is perfectly legal for a wine claim to be a single varietal even if it's only 75% of said variety. Still, my sophisticated wine-writer palette also detected hints of Jungle Juice, unwashed hair and shame. The only *terrior* – earth – I could detect was parking lot asphalt.

When I was in the Middle East, I once drank bootleg whiskey that had been smuggled in country in a heavy plastic IV bags. The plastic did exactly what you expect it to do to the bourbon. I've had brandy made in Serbia and moonshine made in Union County, Mississippi. This was worse.

Standard winespeak simply fails to convey a complete picture because to say that "it lacked subtlety" isn't quite right. There was a very vague feeling that some hag from an early Disney movie had just given me some hexed draught to make me sleep for a hundred years or possibly turn me into a

---

* That's three, right?

goat-man. So, in that regard, I suppose we could call it "enchanting."

The vintners recommend pairing it with a "spicy meat dish" and this is good advice. The operative word here is *spicy*. I'd recommend a spoonful of that Sambol Oelek chili paste or some other condiment that the Vietnamese invented to stick it to the French colonists.

As an optimist, I try to find the silver lining in these things. If you have children in the house and you'd like to throw them off the road to under-age drinking, stock the liquor cabinet with Burlwood – at $2.99 get as many bottles as you need. When the little knee-biters inevitably raid the cellar to experiment, they'll probably develop a lifelong and vaguely Spartan fear of booze. Either that or they'll turn to the harder stuff. You never can tell with children.

In sum, I'll only give it three stars.

How to Drink Champagne

For a drink with such a flouncy reputation, champagne and sparkling wines can be useful these days when properly applied. And applied regularly. The proper application – aside from weddings, IPO's, St. George's day and the odd divorce – is with oysters or a random Saturday lunch. Don't worry about if the month has an "R" in it or not. That was a useful rule of thumb when oysters were harvested into unrefrigerated carts and covered in burlap. The extreme heat of the *R-less* months causes wet oysters to steam themselves slightly open in the cart, whereupon the brine drains away and they get funky. Now they go from bed to refrigerated truck so it doesn't much matter how you spell the month. You might argue that there is more to do on a nice afternoon than a dozen or so oysters, a crisp bottle champagne and the inevitable nap. And you may be right for all I know. Whatever it is, it can wait. Trust me.

In a world awash with Instagram thousandaires pretending to be millionaires, you might be wondering about the price tag. Sparkling wine is a little more sensitive to price – the real Champagnes certainly are. Again, develop the working palette for the stuff, and you can find some pleasant surprises.

The first time I splashed out on a good bottle of Champagne was a bottle of Veuve Cliquot. I didn't get there via a sommelier or because the Queen of England favors it, but because that's what the literary James Bond* drank, as often as not with scrambled eggs. My reasoning had less to do with the character of Bond, and more to do with what I knew about the man who created him. I reckoned that Ian Fleming, something of a well-heeled soak, would know the good stuff. He did. A bottle of VC Brut is going to set you back $65 or so. If you are neither James Bond nor Ian Fleming nor Her Majesty, that might be more than you are looking to spend, but it's a great champagne, even for the price.

In the same range is Pol Roger, a favorite of Winston Churchill – another cash-strapped aristocrat willing to suffer the best of everything. He drank it at lunch everyday and saved Western Civilization from itself. Who knows if the connection is causal or casual, but there we are. The company even created the spilt for him and later named a commemorative wine after the man, which is a hell of a loyalty program. He was hell of a customer.

Dropping down the price list can be risky as it the available wine in the clutches of engagement parties and New Year's Eve. Still, there are options. Back when Earnest Hemingway was an ex-pat living on the confines of his first wife's trust fund, he drank gallons of Spanish sparkling wine

---

* I really can't apologize enough for this.

while he was on hunting and fishing trips, sleeping with married women, and hectoring poor Scott Fitzgerald with all that fizzy "hard business of being a man" foolishness. And I suppose that it *is* tricky to find a second wife with a trust fund.

A bottle of Freixent, from the Penedès region of Spain, will cost you closer to $15. This is important because now this cavalier oyster and champagne afternoon for two you've got planned is costing you less than lunch at any semi-trendy gastro-pub in the city. If this is somehow beneath you, then you don't need me to tell you how to spend your Saturdays.

The Spanish sparkling wines are going to be cheaper than those made in the Champagne region because you can't legally call them Champagne. The same for California bubbles. The French are very French about this. Remember, though, that's marketing, not *necessarily* quality. There are dry sparkling wines that do not have that sickeningly sweetness of those *New Years Eve with 2,500 of Your Closest Friends* bubblies. So, channel your inner "Papa" Hemingway, but don't go pestering farm animals.

Don't forget the Italians, if we're going wide: Prosecco is all the rage, and with good reason, although it's a little sweet for me. Asti Spumante has a terrible reputation dating back to the seventies. But in the seventies all those Italian reds were pretty brutal too. Just revisit the issue from time to time, and see what fits. In short, don't worry too much about price but understand that on the bottom shelve your margin of error widens considerably.

I can't even recall the name of the finest bottle of Champagne I ever had, although I remember the night we drank it very well. A friend in the wine business had just gotten engaged, so he opened a special bottle for the occasion. I remember him explaining to the table that the heavy, sour "breadiness" was a sign of really good Champagne. Someone said it tasted like play-doh, and she wasn't far off, either. That, he said, was a sign of quality and quickly pointed out the proper circumference of the bubbles. A couple of us started singing Don Ho's *Tiny Bubbles*, but he didn't appreciate our crooning.

Still, the sign of truly great champagne isn't that you've been lectured into liking it, but that you look forward to drinking it again.

On a Saturday. With oysters.

SEE THRUS:

UNCLE JOE'S VODKA

For Americans, toasts are for weddings. In that part of the world that used to be snuggled up safely behind the iron curtain, the criteria are a little wider: a) booze is within reach and b) you've made eye contact with another mammal.

Just before the Russians melted into Ukraine in that charming way they did, I found myself at a long, lubricated dinner in Kharkov, a city about 19 miles from the Russian border. We'd gotten into the toasts. I tried my best to sop things up with handfuls of rich black bread spread with, in lieu of butter, duck fat.* The toasts just kept coming, poured out into tiny glasses in endless rounds of something called *pertsivka*. "What is *pertsivka*?" I asked, taking cover behind a lump of black bread.

"It's *horillka* made with hot pepper for spice."

"Great. What's *horillka*?

---

* It was delicious, by the way, but I had to fly home to ask my little brother – a chef – if it had really been delicious or had a phalanx of Slavs beaten me senseless with vodka. He assured me that duck fat is a beautiful thing, no matter how pie-eyed you get.

This amused my host. "It is what Americans call vodka because you don't know the difference.

The man had a point, and he was a doctor. What we call vodka actually came out of Germany in the tenth century, about the time distillation really took off in Europe. In Eastern Europe and Scandinavia, they've always had local varieties of the stuff, and these are often lightly flavored. The *pertsivka* did not taste like vodka with tabasco in it, it was more subtle than that. And it was a joy.

All of these local variants have local names. The term "vodka" means something like "little water" in Russian. It's orderless and tasteless and ironically took hold in the United States in the 1950s as a marketing catch-all because we associated it with the Russians who were scaring the pants off of us at the time.

In college, I knew a guy whose family owned a vodka distillery in Wisconsin. I asked him the name so I could buy a bottle. He gave me one of those "I could tell you but you'd never find it" answers. He wasn't being a snob, just the opposite, he was showing that grim Slavic realism of the firm's natural market. Not only was their entire business in eastern Europe, they didn't even bottle the stuff, it was sold it in six-packs of 12 oz cans. To put this in context, one once of liquor generally has about the same alcohol as a single beer. Each can, which couldn't be resealed, had the same alcohol as a 12 pack of beer. I think that you see the problem.

To the trained ear, Dutch sounds like a Swede trying to speak German. I don't speak Dutch, but I found if I spoke German slowly and badly enough my semi-comic gibberish forced airport personnel to respond in English. I mention this because it wasn't until I was in Amsterdam's Schiphol airport, looking at my boarding pass for the four-hour connecting flight to Kiev, Ukraine, and knowing that after that there was still another one hour connect to Kharkov that I did the math in my head. It took a nine hours to cross the Atlantic from Detroit to Amsterdam. It was going to take another five to get to Kharkov. That's when I realized exactly how far out in the sticks I was headed.

You can always see the lingering impression — like handcuffs ratcheted too tight — when arriving in a place that used to be behind the Iron Curtain. The name Ukraine is a corruption of an old Polish world meaning "borderlands." For the last 1,000 years, everyone who has ruled this beautiful, fertile land considered it just some dumpy non-place. For most of their history even the locals referred to themselves as *Tuteshni*, which means sensibly enough, "the locals."

In Kiev, I was inexplicably bumped to first class on my final one hour Ukrainian Airlines flight to Kharkov. This bit of good luck allowed me to wait out the next six hours of delays in the VIP lounge with a tall, stick-thin woman in a velour track suit that probably cost as much as my favorite shotgun. Eventually we boarded an Antonov 148-100, a 78 passenger commuter jet that, thanks to Soviet era design, still managed to look hulking. The eight first-class seats were wide and comfy and the stewardess looked like a Bond girl.* After 13 hours in a sandwich seat, and another six of delays in the

---

* I don't know that this one counts.

Kiev airport, this fantastic creature looked at me and asked, in heavily accented but otherwise perfect English, if I'd like some brandy with my coffee. I sort of remember saying something cool like, "Why, that would be lovely." But I also sort of remember fairly screaming in her face, "Boy howdy! Would I?" In the throes of euphoria, who can tell about these things?

I got to Kharkov long after dark. A local photographer I'll call Irina and her mother left a sushi bar to pick me up. The place isn't all vodka, bears and furry hats. Nowadays its vodka and a lot of other stuff, like sushi. At night, if you are tired, it can be beautiful. The streets are wide and public spaces enormous. The buildings that pre-date the Soviets and survived the world war are glorious — by night. Irena assured me that not all of Kharkov is like this.

It's not. In the daylight the place can be dismal — and it's a very Bolshevik kind of dismal. How the Soviets managed to make something so boring look so sinister at the same time is a mystery to me. Apartment buildings take up entire city blocks and have absolutely no regard, to the point of aggressive denial, of the humans living there. In mad juxtaposition, the trees and bushes that line the sidewalks are wild and unkempt in some counter-offensive to the standardization of the buildings. Marxists have a desperate sort of love affair with heavy industry as a quantifiable testament to standardization; a system that requires countless cogs and only a few lever pullers. Like America's rustbelt, the people in the East have an almost suicidal nostalgia for a manufacturing golden age whose lack of adaptability is the main cause for said golden age's collapse.

What summed up Kharkov for me more than anything else, aside from the nightly force-feedings of *pertsivka*, was being packed into a local bus like a bunch of sardines. No one spoke much and having exhausted my four words of Ukrainian, it wouldn't have mattered if they had. I was standing near the back and the lady in front of me stuck her palm out to me. She was just a passenger, but it looked like she wanted me to pay my fare. I gave her the money, she handed it to the fella in front of her and the money got passed, in full, to the driver who plopped it in his fare box. I'm not sure what series of unfortunate events would compel me to even get on a Memphis City bus, much less hand my fare over to some random person sitting next to me. This seemed to be the standard procedure, and it worked well enough.

I was contemplating this when I looked out the window and saw a kid, an underfed tween, walking along the street with a 16 oz bottle of beer and an unlit cigarette hanging from his mouth. He was so small the bottle looked like a liter, and yet walked up to a policeman, had a friendly chat as the cop lit the knee biter's cigarette. He took a righteous pull on the lung dart and he and his beer went on their merry way. I looked around the bus and quickly realized that I was the only one on the bus who thought the scene was even noteworthy

Like most grim places, Kharkov wasn't without its sense of humor: Old Soviet era posters and images are used to roughly the same kitschy affect that American use the stylized images of the 1950's. I asked Irina, a member of what is called the Independence Generation – those Ukrainians who have no real memory of the socialist era – about the transformation of the old Soviet big brother spy state into a cartoon. "I remember nothing of the Soviets." She said with a disinterested shrug.

"What about your mother, does she talk about it?"

"I suppose." The only thing a millennial finds less boring than a foreign journalist, apparently, is her mother. In short, the very real danger posed by a government suppressing all of human individuality into a collective economic puree had, in one generation, become the local variant on America's "gramps walking to school uphill both ways" story.

I asked if she was worried that the government was still spying on the people. She seemed genuinely amused that I thought the politicos in Kiev were competent enough to pull off a spy program or, for that matter, had a desire to do anything other than get rich. She waved her smartphone at me, "Everyone knows where I am anyway."

Ukraine got its independence from the USSR in the big eastern bloc bust-up of the early 90's. The country avoided a pesky power vacuum when the entire government quit the communist party *en masse* and got themselves elected, almost to a man, back into the halls of power. This also managed to avoid any fresh blood. The end result is that old habits die hard.

Dinners in this part of the world are lousy with toasts. Not the largely symbolic touching a drink to your lips like we do in the West, either. Over here it's a proper shot. Spend any time here and it's easy to see why. It's hard to get to the human truth of the matter without the drinking to break down the inhibitions in what is essentially a paranoid state. It is a perverse sort of short-term trust in a bottle. The problem is that it also fuels the paranoia in a place where politics is a bloodsport. This can be problematic.

Joseph Stalin, something of a paranoid big government guy, repealed Russia's vodka ban so that he could fund all that grim soviet architecture along with an archipelago of gulags.* Stalin was the first of a line of Soviet premiers who used the time honored tradition of toasting as a weapon of political control. Khrushchev, Stalin's successor, was also notorious for inviting his inner-circle to all night dinners with round after endless round as a deranged truth serum that also had the knock-on effect of throwing all potential rivals off their game. The current Big Cheese, it was always rumored, got his glass refreshed with water.

The Russians could get away with it because this full-contact toasting was just part of the culture. Today, partly thanks to Uncle Joe's foresight is repealing the vodka ban that got the old Tzar shot-up, roughly 25% of Russians die of alcohol related deaths.

F or my part, I was attached to an international aid mission, flying into the neighborhood to perform heart surgery on children, so dinner wasn't adversarial. We drank and talked about the East and the West over *pertsivka*, beer, sausages and cigars. We talked about the Russians and their looming influence, communism and capitalism and the savage tribalism of what we'd call stateside "identity politics"

---

* I hate to be unoriginal in my descriptions but Aleksandr Solzhenitsyn hit the nail on the head.

in a country where, to me at any rate, everyone looked like first cousins. We drank to each other and threw questions around the table and answered them honestly. Why not, we were too drunk to lie well. Then – God's Holy trousers! – no one got bent out of shape. We were drinking to lives being saved (yeah!!!), the Russians were set to invade (boo!!!) and the eastern half of the country knew it (yikes!!!). The only tension came from the fact that because I wasn't a doctor, had recently come from the Middle East, and was wearing what was apparently the only blue blazer east of the Dnieper River, they though I knew something about the Russian business (I didn't).

As I got up to make my exit, I was sure that we'd made progress. So much so that looking back on my notes, I appear to have started writing in the Cyrillic alphabet. Or was that Arabic? Does Chines even *have* a cursive? It's hard to tell. We'd fixed the problem together, of that I was sure. We *had* a solution if the world would just give us time. Too bad none of us can remember what it was.

I've never really had strong opinions about vodka for the simple reason that being (theoretically) odorless and tasteless, I've never quite sure about what, exactly, I was supposed to have an opinion. After the *horillka*, I developed a few, quickly. While two whiskies will taste very different, with vodka – generally an unblended, unaged grain spirit – it's more a matter of texture: harsh v. smooth. Dark Eyes doesn't taste much different from Belvedere, but one burns going down and the other slides home without watering the eyes.

For their part, the Russians aren't nearly as pedantic about their national tipple as the French are about wine or we are about bourbon. They drink so much of the stuff that they'll make it out of just about anything: Potatoes, grain, vegetables, or as in one famous case, the dried fruits and nuts sourced from a what a Moscow zookeeper should have been feeding the monkeys. It hardly mattered because under the Soviets, all the decent vodka was sold abroad as Marx slowly turned in his grave.

You won't find anything called *pertsivka* stateside (I've tried), but you can find hot pepper vodka. It may be as good as the stuff I drank in Kharkov, hell, it might be better. I really wouldn't know. You see, when drinking, context matters.

There are a lot of vodkas made in different ways these days. Belvedere is made from rye in Poland, and again, it goes down smooth. A French vodka – Cîroc – is made from "Five different" grapes and is absolutely worth a try. Grain based Dark Eyes, on the other hand, is out of St. Louis and is absolutely not. Smirnoff, the best-selling vodka in the world, is actually British, but distilled almost anywhere it has a market. I've had a vodka made in Mississippi with rice. It tasted like sake. I can't recommend it.

Being relatively free of those magical impurities picked up from barrel aging, vodka has a reputation of being easier on the hangover. True enough, but it will still dehydrate you as fast as any other spirit. Stir in those sugary mixers (I'm looking at you, Moscow Mule) and it will give your headache a boom that brown water could only dream about.

In Ukraine, they drink the stuff neat (and at home, out of cans). The closest American equivalent is the very dry vodka martini, which is less a cocktail that a cold hooker of vodka with a garnish. My only real issue is that the vodka martini is another case of Americans misnaming things. This concoction called a Kangaroo. The reason we call it a vodka martini is that not even Sean Connery could order a "Kangaroo, shaken, not stirred" and make it sound cool.*

The Cosmopolitan, however, is a different story. As near as I can tell its popularity affectively dates back to somewhere in the middle of the first season of HBO's 90's hit *Sex and the City*. Or at least that's when it went neuvo-icon. According to bartender and author Gary Regan, it was invented by Cheryl Cook in a Miami bar in South Beach called The Strand. It's always been made with vodka...

---

* There was no avoiding this one.

The Cosmopolitan
1 ½ oz Citrus vodka
1 oz Cointreau
½ oz lime juice
¼ oz cranberry juice

Throw all of the above in a shaker with ice, take it a few laps and strain into a cocktail glass. Garnish with a lime wedge.

Pull on a $750 pair of shoes, switch on *Sex and the City* and dream about an implausible life you'll never have.

I have no idea if cosmos are any good for the simple reason that no editor has ever asked my opinion on them. Although, I've made more than I can count.

Back when the charming Mrs. M was still the delightful Ms. C, she worked for a museum and was throwing a hep cocktail party serving martinis and cosmos. I assume she was hoping to get the partiers gassed enough to get cavalier with their bank accounts, but not so gassed that couldn't sign the check.

As it was, the bartenders failed to show up so as the dutiful boyfriend I was pressed into manning one bar. Once a bartender, always a bartender. Soon I was slinging cocktails with expert, if slightly wild, abandon. Or I was until, while slicing a lime, managed to run the knife through my thumb. It was a gusher.

At the time, I was still in investment banking, and one of the ladies at the bank had recently told me an awful internet tale she'd read concerning   someone cutting their thumb while slicing fruit, contracting gangrene and losing said thumb. Hell if I know it was a true story, but I'd had just enough to stir some paranoia. So, I poured out a shot of vodka into a clean cocktail glass and sterilized the wound. It's painful but effective.

It really was an epic party. Never one to abandon my post in the fog of battle, I kept making drinks, wrapping the injured digit on a bev-nap. And because bars are fundamentally gross, I would change these periodically with a quick vodka bath between. I'll admit I was starting to feel light-headed when Ms. C showed back up with a box of band-aids saying something like, "My sister said you were bleeding all over the place." Which just might have been the moment that I thought Ms. C needed to be Mrs. M if she knew what was good for …well me.

So it was that while dressing my digit, some partier swooped around me to pick up what she thought was a pre-mixed cosmo. I was turning around to give my thumb a final booze bath before applying a real bandage when I saw her scooting away. I leapt from the bar, snatched the drink out of her hand and replaced it with another cosmo.

What I'd saved the young lady from was my first every on-the-fly entirely accidental experiment in combat mixology. To wit:

<u>Vlad the Impaler</u>:
4 oz room temperature "fundraiser" vodka
A horribly slashed thumb (mostly attached)

Pour vodka into clean glass and soak horribly slashed thumb until the contents starts to look like a refreshing cosmopolitan.

Richard Murff

GIN PUSS, BAD MEDICINE
& THE COMMODITIES MARKET

T he Russians weren't the only ones to use booze
to their own ends. They were a little meaner
about it, but certainly not alone. The demand
for spirits in Europe became so stable that the monarchs used
them to end famine and to hedge against food shortages.
Sure, the side-effects were pretty lively, but the general plan
did what it was supposed to do.

In a society without modern transportation and shipping,
a bad harvest is a tricky problem. They were relatively rare,
but when happened it was an ugly sort of zaniness that
ensues, particularly in urban areas. Kings were always
looking around for diverse forms of carbohydrates, but this
was trickier than it sounds: Farmers, being a practical lot,
only grow as much grain as they can eat and sell. To grow a
surplus not only means unsold inventory, but that the price
on what they do sell will go down. The end result is that
there isn't much surplus on a good year, but when a crop
failure happens the price of grain, when you can get it, sky
rockets. The farmer will make his money either way because
even if he loses half his crop, he sells it for twice the price.
Practically, then, asking a farmer to create a surplus to keep

prices down in the both good years and lean, is a low percentage thing to do. For the urban poor, however, high food prices or scarcity is the sort of thing that triggers revolution. In general, kings don't like revolutions and English kings like them even less, as their subjects have always been fairly mellow about that "divine right" foolishness.

You'd be forgiven for wondering just what the hell any of the above has to do with gin. Bear with me.

King James (II of England, and VII of Scotland) was a Scot who, as a Stuart, had inherited the crowns of Scotland, England and Ireland.* To the English, that he was a Scot was mildly annoying. The Catholic thing chapped, but as he'd come to the throne *without* a civil war, they were prepared to let it slide. Up to a point. His protestant nephew, the Duke of Monmouth, launched a rebellion in the south and the Duke of Argyle stirred Clan Campbell up enough to launch one from the north. James made short order of the uprisings, but wanted to keep a larger standing army afterwards. This made people nervous. Then he started carrying on about religious liberty and tolerance, and that was not something the freedom loving English could abide. Certainly not if the papists kept trying to blow up Parliament. James may have been devout, but let's face it, he wasn't a people person.

Things got prickly. The way the ruling class had it sorted, the king may have had a divine right to the crown but so did his daughter from his first marriage, the Protestant Mary,

---

* Three separate countries with one king. What could go wrong? Political unions would come later.

who was living in Holland married to William of Orange. So they invited the King's son-in-law to invade the country and "rescue the nation and religion." James sent three regiments to meet the invaders, all of which defected to the other side, which even the most practical of military leaders would take as a bad omen. William just kept claiming that he was there to secure the wife's inheritance. In 1688, James fled to France and England got William and Mary, a duel monarchy that was properly Protestant. And Dutch.

Willam had seen what food shortages could do, and hatched a plan to create a secondary market for English grain. William reckoned that if he could stimulate gin production, it would expand the market for grain beyond what people ate because the distillers would become a secondary market for grain. Then, so the thinking went, in a year with a blight or a crop failure there would be an excess of grain the cover the food shortage. In short, people might go sober, but they wouldn't go hungry.

This was already happening without central planning in Scotland, but with whisky. Willam was Dutch, didn't want grain surpluses heading north of the border.

The plan would only work, however, only if gin was more popular that beer or wine, or any other spirit. William outlawed brandy and wine from papist France, left the fees and taxes on English brewers,* and let the gin industry run

---

* Whisky, for tax reasons was mainly produced in Scotland & Ireland. The "reason" was that taxes were hard to collect out there in the stix.

amok without any regulation. And it worked. It just worked a little too well.

Now, I'm a free market guy and think that less government pesters people who actually work for a living the better. Still, there is a practical limit to my libertarianism. Gin is basically vodka infused with juniper berries, which had been a medicinal herb for centuries. Unregulated producers and sellers started to repeatedly distill it to the point of being 80% ABV, or 160 proof. Then served it in big beer mugs. Beer, if you're wondering is a whopping 5% ABV. You might think that it killed people. You'd be right, gin was killing people left and right.

Now if the poor were going hungry, it was because they were spending what little money they had on gin. Which, from the royal point of view, is not the sort of hungry that triggers revolutions, but it can still wreck the social order. London was full of uncontrollably rowdy, or comatose, drunks. Worse, many were uncontrollably nude, having sold their clothes for gin. And little naked bastards were showing up all over the place because the hopelessly destitute women were drinking as much as the hopelessly destitute men, but they had one more thing to sell. The whole thing was unseemly.

The English can be a fairly eccentric lot but they are also pretty traditionally minded as well. All the upper classes could see was that the lower classes were uncontrollable, had lost their groveling sense of deference to their social betters, and the nudity was of the entirely wrong sort. It was starting to make the ruling class feel unsafe.

The Gin Act of 1736 was passed, which required a £ 50 license to sell it legally, about £ 12,000 in 2021. This was duly ignored. Without much of a police force, the government tried to use informers to sniff out scofflaws. That worked about as well as you might imagine: The informers weren't so much ostracized as beaten to death by the local booze hounds wanting to get "ginny."

Then a man named Dudley Bradstreet stumbled upon a less dramatic, if much more effective and silly ruse. Even in those days, the English were pretty serious about civil liberties, and a witness had to identify both a name and a face to give testimony in court. Bradstreet created a sort of drive-by gin fountain that came to be known as the Puss & Mew. Basically he rented a house and bought all the gin he could lay his hands on. Near a tightly barred door that was never opened, he installed a fake cat head and an outstretched paw, and spread the word. Soon people were speaking their order into the cat's mouth, then dropping in their money, and holding their glass, bottle, bucket or their gaping pie-hole under the paw, which held a pipe. The chav got their gin and it was more or less impossible for them to testify who it was selling them the stuff.

The problem just seemed to be getting worse and you might be tempted to call William III (he'd died in 1702) a damned fool until the 1750s when the country did suffer a series of crop failures. Over the years, farmers had been growing much more grain than the country ate in order to get it completely legless. The price of gin went up, but the price and supply of bread remained fairly stable.

The government's domestic policy had actually worked, if only at a huge cost in unintended consequences. For one thing the upper classes were now fully aware of what the lower classes would do when massed and drunk. And let's be honest, they would really rather they do it someplace else.

...AND HOW TO DRINK IT

As empires go, the Brits pretty well spanned the globe. It brought fortunes to the mother country, and it also provided a convenient place to send those morons drinking gin out of pussy.

In the 1700's a Scottish doctor by the name of George Cleghorn discovered that quinine could be used to prevent and treat disease because it suppressed parasites in the system. While this was of limited value in a place like Scotland, for a young fellow heading out into the sweltering, pestilent Empire east of Suez, it might just save his life. At least that was the theory.

Quinine was added to soda water to make it into a health "tonic." The stuff was still bitter tasting, so sugar was added. Then lime. And the daily gin ration because, well, wouldn't you?

Dr. Cleghorn's findings were correct *in theory*. In practice, you'd need to drastically up the quinine dosage to actually do any good. At the favored gin to tonic ratio you'd have to be half-in-the-bag from dawn till dusk to, according to one 2004 study, reach "the lower level of therapeutic efficiency."

The result was one of the greatest hot weather drinks/ dubious malaria retardants in the bleary history of cocktails:

The gin and tonic. You are one torrential downpour from a Graham Greene novel.

Modern, commercial tonic has even less medicinal value and has been sweetened into a soft drink. Years ago, even before the "Vlad the Impaler" situation, when I first started dating the charming Ms. C. We were having cocktails over at my future in-law's house where they were lining up the gin *and sodas*. Because I was new, after a long search someone produced a faded bottle tonic water. It looked dusty. I said I'd take it however the house made it.

Quickly I found that I couldn't go back to old standard G&T – it was too sweet, too cloying. I wanted to suck the enamel off my teeth. Plenty of higher end tonics have come out since, and they are better, I've never warmed to them.

I settled on a classic tonic syrup made by the good people at the Jack Rudy Cocktail Company. It is, more or less, a quinine concentrate in a simple syrup of cane sugar and some flavorful botanicals. A teaspoon (about a third of what the recipe actually calls for) into some gin on ice, a lime, and topped off with soda, and this, gentle reader, is what you need to be drinking with the mad dogs and Englishmen go out under the noonday sun. The quinine has a light, high bitterness that offsets the sweet, which, it turns out is exactly what is missing from modern G & Ts.

As for the gin, Hendricks was probably the first out of the gate with its botanical forward gin, along with Junipero. These work better in G&T, (or S) than in martinis. Enter the age of a new artisanal gin hitting the market every week, each trying to outdo the other: If more botanicals are good, then a lot more must be better. It's not. One of my personal favorites is Old Dominick's No. 10 – which manages to be interesting without getting so fashionable that it slips into parody.

Which brings us back to the concept of balance; you find whatever works for you. You need a well-balanced gin that is interesting but doesn't make itself obvious, with a tonic that is however you like it. I may not fully understand my wife's choice of beer, but on gin she's right: Give it a twirl in the ice and let it sit before diving in and the botanicals open up and soften.

Gin Fizz

T he Ramos Gin Fizz is one of those great cocktails that we've all heard of but have likely never had. A seemingly bizarre concoction involving egg white, cream, and something called orange flower water, it is a creation that, on paper, makes absolutely no sense but it comes together beautifully. And in that sense, it really is very much a New Orleans creation.

Walker Percy tells a story from when he was in medical school in 1941. He and a nurse were on a date and he ordered a gin fizz at the Boo Snooker bar in the New Yorker Hotel. You can take one look at the thing and see that it has cream in it, but the egg white was a surprise to Percy. He was allergic. His front lip began to stick out to where he could barely speak, much less deliver a serviceable smooch. His eyes swelled shut and then, summoning all his brawny male energy, promptly fainted. The nurse, being a nurse, drove him to Bellevue and gave the him a shot. This was not the gal he'd eventually marry. So do sort out your personal relationship with egg whites before diving into one.

Created by Carl Ramos in 1888 at the Imperial Cabinet Saloon, reportedly he employed several men behind the bar just to shake them, for 12 to 15 minutes. I don't know about that. New Orleans barman Chris Hannah says that 25-45 seconds will do. That, however, is longer than you think.

Light and frothy, this is one of those jazz brunch drinks. Unlike the bloody Mary, thought, I'm not sure I'd want to eat it with anything. There is, in taste, something of a meringue, with the club soda lightening things up in the glass. If you've got a meringue *texture*, you've gone too far with the shaking.

While everyone is trying to put their own twist on classics these days, don't monkey with the recipe. It's so well put together that the whole thing might fall apart if you tinker with it. Even the orange flower water has its place.

The trick is small glasses. If you've got Collins glasses, fine. Pint glasses won't do. For one thing, like the martini, you want it to stay cold. This is a delicate sipper, and you can't really make a batch beforehand. Yes, it's labor intensive but a lot of things worth doing are: A grilled steak, charbroiled oysters, etc. Besides, what's wrong with a little effort when you have something special, interesting and just a little off-kilter?

Again, if you are allergic to egg whites, avoid. As Dr. Percy would attest, there is nothing sophisticated about anaphylactic reactions. To Wit:

<u>Ramos Gin Fizz</u>:
2 oz   gin
.75 oz   simple syrup
.5 oz   heavy cream
.5 oz lemon juice
.5 oz lime juice
3 dashes orange flower water
1 fresh egg white
Club soda, chilled, as a topper

The gin, simple syrup, cream lemon & lime juice, orange flower water, egg white go into a shaker without ice. Shake like a British nanny for 10-15 seconds.

Add ice and shake for another 20-30 seconds. Strain into a Collins (or smaller) glass, and use chilled club soda to rinse the inside of the shaker and pour on as a topper.

I found another recipe that called for putting the club soda in with the shake to keep it from separating, which works better.

Richard Murff

THE MARTINI

The Martini is a strangely controversial drink – its purists are just a little too pedantic for their own good. And I know this because I've never been able to mix one that really hit the spot. A guy that I've sailed with for years makes a near a perfect one nearly every time and to make matters worse, Capitan Bill isn't stingy with his recipe, "It's just math: Four parts gin to one part vermouth." It's not that simple though, and Bill knows it because invariably he walks the solid math back to something *close* to five parts gin. *But not quite.*

Well, that's simple enough, except that it isn't.

First, avoid cheap gins. If you are on a budget, or in between royalty checks, Barton Gin lives on the bottom shelf and routinely wins blind tastings. Even with good gin, though, tastes vary. A lot. Really floral gins are everywhere these days, but they don't really lend themselves to a martini. Tanqueray, for our purposes, is a hard one to beat because it will let the vermouth shine through. Hayman London Dry is another great choice.

While gin is the main actor in a martini, in its supporting role, the vermouth can make or break the production. Martini & Rossi is great classic go-to, although I prefer

174

Dolan. Some white vermouths have a yellowish tint which may not offend the taste but, like diamonds, you want your martini to stay crystal clear.

The real pothole with vermouth comes in where you store it: *Vermouth must be refrigerated*. It's a fortified white wine, but it is white wine so it goes off. The reason people want super dry martinis is that most people – including those behind the bar who should know better – are making their cocktails with rancid vermouth. And a martini, made to Capitan Bill's specs, with fresh vermouth, is an entirely different creature that the cocktail that you think you know.

So stow it in the fridge and it'll keep for about a month or so, and after that use it for cooking. If you aren't cooking with wine, then you really need to be. But that's another book.

The other tip, and I really have know idea why this should matter if the math is constant, is that it is easier to make four martinis than one. Shake or stir them up, pour your drink, and strain the rest into a small pitcher to stow in the fridge to avoid dilution. Which is fine if people are coming over but a bit of a commitment on a Tuesday night.

Some variants:

Captain Bill's Martini:
4 parts gin (or really 5, but not quite... it's complicated)
1 part vermouth
Olive
Lemon twist

Throw it all in a shaker and do it's thing. Pour into glass, preferable chilled but not necessary. Garish with olive and lemon twist.

Hoffman House Martini:
8 parts gin
1 part dry vermouth
3 to 5 dashes orange bitters
Cocktail olive

Combine, shake, serve – garnish with olive. A little different, but hard to beat.

Vesper (the James Bond Martini)*:
3 parts Gordon's gin
1 vodka
1 part kino lillet
Lemon twist

Combine and shake, don't stir, over ice and strain into glass and garnish with a thin slice of lemon.

For maximum effect you'll to be in better shape then you actually are. You aren't that charming, but you'll need to be. If not the fate of the world, at least an US bail-out of MI6 should hang in the balance. You will almost certainly be getting your ashes dragged later.

Mr. C's Martini:
A "special occasion" martini in memory of a hell of a guy I worked with at an investment firm. Like me, his

* And this is the pay-off. Now you too can make a vesper.

personality was near polar opposite of the successful investment banker and yet, unlike me, he was successful at it. When he told me the recipe, his eyes gleamed.

- •4 parts gin
- •1 part vermouth
- •2 Blue cheese stuffed olives
- •More blue cheese

Mix in a shaker the usual way and pour over olives. Using a very fine grater, take a single pass overhead with the blue cheese so that "it drifts onto the surface like snow."

No wonder the man's eyes gleamed.

WORLD WAR II IN A COCKTAIL GLASS:

Despite all the "whispering vermouth over the gin "nonsense, there is no Churchill martini because he thought that the cocktail was "barbaric." He was more of a whisky/brandy/champagne/G&T/port guy. Which really should be enough. FDR, on the other hand, loved a see-thru"

FDR Martini:

2 parts gin
1 part vermouth
1 teaspoon olive brine
Lemon twist
Cocktail olive

Take the lemon twist around the rim of a chilled glass. Combine gin, vermouth and olive brine in a cocktail shaker with ice and shake well. Strain into and garnish with olive."

Hitler, for his part, had no signature martini. The man was a teetotal. Draw your own conclusions.

Richard Murff

RUM:
THE DARKNESS & THE LIGHT

Rum is the spirit world's switch hitter – and perhaps more than any other liquor encompasses the troubled duality of man. Although, I'm not sure I'd stick that on the bottle.

Old school dark rum is the stuff of prison colonies, forced labor, and drunken sailors – who are a little of both. And slavery. You can't get around that one. With some refinement you find yourself with a lighter, see-thru version with it's little paper umbrellas, island paradises and a spanking Jimmy Buffet soundtrack.

If ye olde rum drinkers died of scurvy and malaria, the next generation is going to get it with melanoma, ridiculous wardrobe violations and being trampled by enthusiastic Parrotheads.

Rum didn't always have that exotic vibe. It was American's liquor long before we got sideways with the Europeans still marauding around the Caribbean. The Spirit of 76, then, was rum. Then we realized we were sitting on more corn, wheat, rye than we knew what to do with. Unlike whiskies, vodkas, or brandy, Rum isn't made from grain or grape but cane sugar or molasses. If you are really a DYI sort, you can make rum out of brown sugar. Let me know how that turns out.

New England used to be lousy with rum distilleries - like Kentucky is with bourbon today. But the raw material, molasses, had to be imported from the Caribbean. Perhaps this gave it a vaguely nautical and exotic air, because rum, for reasons I can't explain and more than any other liquor, seems to be a matter of lifestyle choice. What the modern rum drinker is looking for are pirates and high-seas adventure. Or, at the very least, deep-sea fishing.

So it was that I was standing inside the Cruzan Rum distillery in St. Croix, US Virgin Islands. It's actually owned by Beam Suntory, the Japanese firm that owns Jim Beam, but it sure as hell doesn't look like billion dollar multi-national. It looks like a Caribbean rum distillery on a pretty little island existing somewhere between US statehood and a colony. Which is exactly where it is. The current architecture of the place is what we'd call mid-century sensible, but there has been a rum distillery on this site since 1760.

St. Croix is a jewel of an island, and it certainly makes you want to drink rum rather than, say bourbon. Certainly not Scotch. It isn't the heat either. It's no hotter there than in Memphis, and with a tropic breeze, it's a damn site less humid. Yet there is something hard-wired into our drunk monkey that when we get to a zip code that includes beaches or marinas we start thinking, "*Well, yo ho ho indeed. It's a bottle of rhum methinks.*" Ridiculous and flamboyant shirts are pulled from the back of the closet. We stop shaving. Baths get, well, irregular. Rum causes us to go full Fletcher Christian on ourselves.

I like the odd martini myself, but drinking one has never triggered my to start carrying on like James Bond*, David Niven or even my Father-in-Law. Drinking Scotch doesn't make me pine to go stalking Highlands stags – I already want to do that. If I go any amount of time away from the ocean or a sailboat, I never think about rum. Certainly not enough to go around spelling with that spare "h" the way that they do in Haiti. It's hard to say why, other than an unsung element in booze is context.

It may be that we associate it with places were sugar cane grows, and if you aren't from a tropical climate, it is exotic. That's fine, but if you want to keep it jolly I wouldn't focus on how sugar cane is harvested. The plant isn't indigenous to the Caribbean, but was introduced to the region when Columbus was trying to find a way to India and China without dealing with the Arabs. What he found, among other things, was an island called Ay Ay by the people who lived there, who were called themselves Kalinago. Without running by the locals, Columbus renamed the island *Isla de la Santa Cruz* (Island of the Holy Cross) in 1492 and it was there that the first conflict between Europeans and the locals took place. Although I don't think it was over naming rights. The Spanish did not, however, colonize the island. Their personal hygiene was revolting enough that the diseases they carried

---

* Eight, if you're still counting.

killed off the local population so thoroughly that less than a century later, the island was entirely uninhabited.

It wouldn't stay that way. Dutch and English and French settlers showed up in St. Croix in 1625, then the English threw the Dutch and the French out. The Spanish showed up again and expelled the English in 1650 and then French came back in force in 1651 and hung around until they evacuated the island in 1698. It remained uninhabited for 38 years.

The Danish East India company bought the island in 1733 and they introduced sugar cane because by this time everyone realized that it grew like wild fire in the climate and there were fortunes to be made. This was great news for the Europeans who were mad for the stuff and were in the process of inventing global trade and diabetes. It is hard to oversell exactly how much the Columbian exchange, goods criss-crossing from old world to new and vice versa, changed European food. The tomato, that staple of Italian cuisine, is an American transplant,. So is corn, chili peppers, peanuts, the lowly potato and cacao – or chocolate.

All that sugar money wasn't coming from rum. It was coming from a form of sugar that would granulate. When milling sugar cane, another awful process, one of the by-products is a syrupy liquid called molasses. Which is basically the starter kit for rum. This led to the infamous "Triangular Trade" that ran for some 300 years. Textiles and other European products were shipped to Africa, where they were traded for slaves at market. Slaves were shipped to the Caribbean and US to work on plantations (the death rate in the sugar plantations being worse that the other appalling death rates). Caribbean sugar and molasses was shipped to distillers in the US, and then raw goods like sugar and cotton and finished rum were shipped to Europe and the loop started again.

In return for its trouble, the new world got sugar-cane. They'd have been better off without it. It may grow well under the right conditions but harvest the cane on anything like a commercial scale in a pre-industrial society was such a terrible, labor-intensive operation that you literally couldn't pay people to do it. It was worse than death. Scratch that, it was almost synonymous with death. This led to slavery – which is terrible and impossible to justify. And *that* led to slave revolts – which were also terrible in their violence but, on balance, fairly easy to justify. Slave revolts led to emancipation – which is wonderful and has no need for justification. It also led to post-revolt massacres, which were less so.

Which is not to say that it was all rum punch after that. Inspired by the ideals of the French Revolution and the Rights of Man, the slaves of Haiti, led by General Toussaint L'Ouverture, a former slave and the first black general of the French Army, revolted against the Motherland.

Faced with a revolt in the colonies and that the slavery itself was at so obviously at odds with the revolutionary ideals at home, France's First Republic abolished slavery in its colonies. Or rather, in a sort of bureaucratic hedge, most of them. Satisfied, L'Ouverture pledged allegiance to France and became Haiti's Governor General.

By 1802, back in Paris, some of the more absurd parts of the revolution were proving unsustainable and the country found itself thinking that Napoleon Bonaparte was the way to go. It's hard to say if the general population thought this, Napoleon Bonaparte certainly thought that it was the way to go. He took one look at Haiti and saw a colony that had gone from wildly profitable to not remotely so. He reintroduced slavery because, well, the man was an ass.

When L'Ouverture got word, he declared himself Governor-General for life, which may have been an indirect way to declare independence. Napoleon needed the sugar money, so sent an army to show L'Ouverture who was calling the shots. The French Army was promptly decimated.

I like an underdog as much as the next guy, but it was yellow fever, not the Haitians that pole-axed the French forces. Still, a win is a win. In 1803, Haiti became the second republic in the hemisphere and the first to be established out of a slave revolt. In 1804, the massacre of the whites was ordered and the plantation system was promptly re-instated. This time for wages (theoretically). That's not as gracious as it appears, the peasants still had no choice in the matter. The place just wouldn't run without the sugar harvest.

Something like that happens and word will spread. After an 1848 slave revolt in St. Croix, the island's slaves were emancipated – which led to the same old problem for Denmark as it had for France and then Haiti. The Danish solution was to enact a law saying if the new freedmen wanted to work, employment contracts would bind them and their entire family to the land. This led to the 1878 St. Croix labor riots which were destructive but didn't change much. Some thirty six years later, in 1916, the US bought the island for $25 million dollars.

Caribbean history is a tricky mess to sort out. Sticky too, like molasses. Once the US bought St. Croix, it hitched its star to vacation paradises and petrochemical refinement. Haiti, however, is simply another mess. Somehow, despite its grim history and the countries inability to produce something as simple as a domestic lightbulb, they still make damn good rum. At least they make one damn good rum. Rhum Barbancourt 15 is regarded as one of the world's best of its kind. That's it's made in Port Au Prince may defy logic, but perhaps not history.

Sadly, if you clomp around Latin America you run into a lot of really good rums made in countries that don't produce much else. I have a soft spot for Flor de Caña, made in Nicaragua. While in Managua, I managed to run smack into in what they call "social unrest" down there. The story would be a lot better if I hadn't been using my father as interpreter — he grounded me from going to the riot. Which is why you should never take your father on assignment.

Still, Flora de Caña always makes me a tad nostalgic.

HOW TO MAKE GROG

Rum though, isn't a Caribbean thing, it's a far-flung, sea-faring *exotic* thing. The British may have been turned out of St. Croix, but they sure as hell turned up just about everywhere else. The British navy wasn't the only imperial fleet whose sailors were given fairly generous rations of ale, about the only generous thing in a sailor's life. For the British navy, ale rations worked well enough for relatively short jaunts around European waters or even the northern crossing to America, where the entire ocean acted as a refrigerator. Further afield those huge casks of ale became problematic: They took up too much room and without mother nature acting as your cooling system, the ale tended to spoil in the heat.

The issue was partially solved by Sister Hildebrand's innovation of dramatically upping the hops as a natural preservative to stop spoilage *en route* to the boys in India. Delicious and refreshing, what came to be known as India Pale Ale still took up too much room on long journeys to the far corners of the empire.

Alcoholically speaking, rum takes up a lot less storage space per dram than beer and doesn't spoil. Hence the British navy's fabled Rum Ration. Old naval lore is drowning in the stuff – Churchill never made the "Rum, sodomy and the lash" quip, but *someone* did. The Admiralty didn't officially abolish the sailor's daily rum ration until 1971.

In a boozy counter-point to American's failed Whiskey Rebellion of 1791-94, Australia's Rum Rebellion, in 1808, was more or less successful. And for those of you who like your Vegemite served with a side of irony: Australia had been originally envisioned as a colony with neither booze nor the money with which to buy it. The theory, conceived by one Lord Sydney, was that all those gin-soaked poor people running amok in London were their regrettable, criminal selves due to want of both booze and money. He thought that if you took away both you'd have cracked the nut of a civil society. Or at least a manageable underclass. This, admittedly, was a hard sell. No one was voluntarily going to a land with neither cocktail hour nor money, anymore than they were going to sign up for the sugar harvest. So the Crown sent convicts who didn't have a say in the matter.

There were, of course, a couple of logistical issues. For one thing, you just can't walk to Australia from anyplace that isn't Australia. You must hire a ship or three, along with the crew, to haul your social experiment to the far side of the planet where, presumably, they'd stop pestering Lord Sydney on his way to the opera. The sailors, though, *did* have a say in the matter, so they were a) damn well going to get paid, with money thank you very much, and b) they were going to have rum for the journey.

The another flawed element in the plan was that unless you guard them very closely, convicts tend to not show up at the rendezvous the law enforcement establishment likes to dictate. They'll just wander off, they really will. So Royal Marines were sent to guard the prisoners. These particular Royal Marines, it's worth noting, weren't elite special ops sorts. Australia was a terrible posting, not the sort of place where careers went to die, they were already DOA. Most of these guys were going down under as plea-bargains from earlier court-martials. Still, they were enlisted and they wanted their rum ration.

Along with the evils of colonization, there is also an awful lot of ink spilt on the evils of money. Money on its own, however, isn't anymore evil that say, a shovel. It's just an instrument. Dig a well with it and you're a hero, hit your mother with it and you're deranged monster. The *want* of money makes us crazy – that's fair – but money is pretty handy for a functioning society. As any society built on forced labor will illustrate.

Lord Sydney wanted to build a classless utopia (well, not for himself, for the regrettable others) and to do that, *someone* has to go the extra mile. Neither convict nor slave is likely to do so. What they are likely to do is exactly two teaspoons less than the required minimum work to stave off death or torture. Without the hope of freedom, promotion or money, why would a rational person do any more than the bare minimum?

And it's right here that Australia comes off its idealistic rails. It was full of ex-cons and ex-prostitutes, two groups not known for their professional ambition. To get them to do anything you had to bribe them. In the absence of hard currency, there was booze in the form of naval rum. And just like in America, liquor became money. So, obviously, to keep a modicum of order, the Marines, had to make more rum. It wasn't a secret, they were know as the Rum Corp.

Now, despite all Sydney's planning to the contrary, his new Utopia had both booze and money in one convenient and easily abused package. On balance, it wasn't a good system, but it did manage to go for about twenty years. It was something of an embarrassment to the Crown.

To get control of the situation, London appointed one William Bligh as Governor of New South Wales. If the name is familiar this is the same William Bligh who commanded the HMS *Bounty* until 1789, when his lieutenant, Fletcher Christian, lead a mutiny on said *Bounty*. The mutineers set the Bligh and the loyal crew adrift in the South Pacific without food, water or topsiders.

The salty bastard survived somehow, and made it some 3,618 nautical miles* in an open boat to the Dutch colony of Timor. In testimony during the Admiralty inquest into the loss of the *Bounty*, some of the loyal crew admitted that during six weeks adrift, that they too considered relieving the man of command. What saved Bligh from a second lifeboat mutiny was that, despite his epic douche-baggery, his skill as a navigator was almost surreal. Evidently, the man was a floating GPS.

In Timor, he fumed about the loss of his first command and wanted to get back to England as fast as possible to get his side of the story out first. Bligh hailed a ride a ship where he was neither an officer nor the navigator, and yet passenger Bligh was so insufferable that the captain of the vessel

---

* Or 4,160 miles. A nautical mile is … you don't care.

threatened to leave him in Cape Town, in South Africa if he didn't cool it.

So naturally, in its wisdom, the Crown appointed him governor of a penal colony.

In no time the Australians, prisoners and "Rum Corps" Marines alike, hated Bligh as much as everyone else who'd ever met the guy. Bligh's problem was that while he could do math like a calculator, he had no imagination. London briefed him to fix the rum problem in Australia, so he made rum illegal. He was the sort of man who thought that would do the trick.

And, presto! Just like that the British Empire had its one and only military successful coup.* The Rum Corp came to Bligh's house were his daughter made a heroic stand at the front door. As it was, the marines got around the girl and found her father hiding under a bed. They arrested the governor and put their own guy in office.

As coups go, this one was pretty modest: No one wanted independence, or even a new head of state, just a governor who knew what the score was in Australia. It's worth noting that in the vast annals of business books, there is not one called *Management Secrets of Captain Bligh*.

You see a lot of "Navy" and "Admiralty" strength rum out there now that everything has gone all craft and authentic. Most of it comes in fantastically designed bottles filled with juice that tastes like rum-flavored

---

* The historical jury is still out on whether what William of Orange did to his father-in-law was a foreign invasion or a *coup d'etat*. The gin thing, however, is all him.

moonshine. Why, you might well ask, did the Admiralty of the world's most powerful navy want to get all their sailors lit up on a daily basis? The short answer is that they didn't. Those jack tars weren't staggering around like Keith Richards with tankards full of 100 proof rum, they were drinking *grog*.

Like a lot of cocktails invented by the British Military/Industrial complex, grog was essentially just spiked medicine. The official Royal Navy recipe was simple: half a barrel of water, half a barrel of rum, and a quart of lime juice. The rum "sterilized" the water, provided a mild pain-killer and antibiotic, and helped the average jack-tar to NOT think about his grim lot in life. The quart of lime juice provided much needed vitamin C that acted as a hedge against scurvy. Thus, extending the sailor's misery until he died of some other horrible trauma.

The problem for the modern drinker is that, if you haven't been press-ganged into the navy, grog is actually awful. So how to make a civilian version?

The first step is to lighten it up: use soda instead of still water, maybe tweek the ration from 1:1 to two-parts water, one-part rum. Give it a good squeeze of lime, more than a twist. You are allowed to say *one* of the following (but not both): "Avast" or "Me'Hearties." Then cut it out.

Use dark rum, it's more interesting. The light stuff has too much of a tikki-torch/ beach party vibe and no sense of adventure.

However, if that's your scene.

THE LIGHTER SIDE

Rum, fortunately, does have a lighter side. Complete with a soundtrack provided by the one and only Jimmy Buffet.* If you don't want to lighten things up quite so much, or wear a parrot as a hat, you do have light rum options that aren't entirely ridiculous.

Ernest Hemingway always moved deeper into the tropics each time he divorced the current wife's trust fund. He drank scads of the stuff. Papa also froze gin into little pellets so he could toss handfuls in his mouth like alcoholic, semi-liquid tic-tacs. Clever, to be sure, but this chapter is about rum.

In 1927, with the success of his boozy *The Sun Also Rises,* he divorced his first wife Hadley's trust fund to marry the much larger private income of a writer for *Vogue* one Pauline Pfeiffer of Pigott, Arkansas. This enabled the couple to honeymoon in the south of France where the universe dealt out some rare, fast-acting karma: Hemingway contracted anthrax. Pauline was pregnant, a condition that makes women both moody and incredibly practical, so she decided that they were moving back to the US. Fashion writer's for

---

* Buffet is from Mobile, which may not sound exotic if you are from the 49 states that aren't Alabama. In state, it's known as "Planet Mobile." Nice people.

Vogue, once stationed in Paris, do not tend to move back to Pigott, Arkansas. She bought a house in Key West, Florida with money from her Uncle Gus. Key West is a rum town and Papa took to the stuff like a fish to water.

Ignoring the advice of his mistress, Martha Gellhorn, Hemingway divorced all of Pauline's stuff and bought a house in Cuba. Gellhorn was another writer and was not independently wealthy, but his career was rolling by this point and Cuba was really cheap. Hemingway always seemed to think that it would be his Spain of the tropics, but that never really panned out. Neither did Martha, who never quite cottoned to that "Papa" business the way he thought a wife should. He moved to another mistress who assumed that the old cod would be more manageable because at his age he liked taking naps alone.

Then Castro's revolution ran the Bacardi rum plant to Puerto Rico and Papa to Ketchum, Idaho.* Castro, for the record, reinvented society as free of the evil land-owners who forced the Cuban peasants to work the sugar cane plantations. At least that was the plan. Castro quickly forced the peasants back onto the plantations for the sugar harvest against their will. To be fair, he sent college students as well, but they were useless in the field and complained too much so they got sent back to the dorm. Castro sold this as necessary to build his socialist paradise where all workers

---

* This isn't as random as it sounds, Ketchum was something of a celebrity haunt back when celebrities felt compelled to act somewhat normal. Jimmy Buffet, I understand, is actually a normal guy.

were equal. Except, of course the poor people working the sugar cane against their will.

God's Holy Trousers! You just can't get away from it!

Whatever else that you think of the man, Hemingway was pretty tight with his prose and plotting. Less so with his personal legend. After returning home from World War I, just what exactly he'd gotten up to while in Italy morphed with alarming speed. He went from the modest reality of being a teenaged civilian Red Cross ambulance driver near the front for a whopping two weeks, to fighting with an elite Italian brigade (which, we are to believe, recruited teenaged American ambulance drivers with no military training). So, it is fitting that even according to legend, the legend of the Papa daiquiri doesn't completely add up.

To begin with, the fact that his favorite drink was a frozen daiquiri is jarring for an aspiring writer to learn. I remember stumbling across this little tidbit as an undergrad at Alabama and thinking something along the lines of "Well, *that* is a little off-brand. I know plenty of people who love a daiquiri but they all belong to sororities. At least the ones who'll admit it. And if she ran afoul of a bear that needed wrestling, or a spider squashed, she'd likely send me and my bottle of cheap Scotch whisky to do the job." In Papa's defense, though, the original daiquiri was not frozen – just very, very cold. What Hemingway drank bears little resemblance to that squealer I recognized from Bourbon Street and spring break.

The tale begins innocently enough with our hero wandering into the El Floridita bar in Havana in search of a bathroom. He was getting older and eating handfuls of gin pellets, so the story holds water this far. There he saw the barman mixing up a batch of daiquiris. By the time Earnest Hemingway had settled in Cuba, he'd already become Papa – that famous devil-may-care cartoon of his former self. He snatched a daiquiri off the bar, gave it a quaff and promptly told the barman what he was doing wrong. As you do. Despite the standard recipe having been published before Papa was born, what *he* thought it needed was to double the rum and lose the sugar. Thus creating what became known as "the Papa Doble."

For reference: here is the original 1898 version

Daiquiri:
2 oz white rum
.25-.5 oz simple syrup
.3 oz lime juice

Shake well with cracked ice and pour into a chilled cocktail glass.

Which wasn't good enough for Papa, so…

The Papa Doble:
4 oz white rum
.3 oz lime juice

As cocktails go, the doble is nether terribly clever or even that good unless you are using very premium white rum, and the smart money is that these guys weren't. And if you are using premium rum, there is no reason to make it quite so cold that it anesthetizes   the tongue. Like the extra dry martini, it's a cold hooker of straight booze with a garnish. Great for getting legless, sure, but a little much for market segment that lacks an entourage of hangers-on to get them home to the put-upon wife.

Hemingway, though, was a better writer than mixologist. The only cocktail recipe he ever published was the Death in the Afternoon named after his eponymous bullfighting book. It was featured in a 1935 celebrity bar book called *So Red the Nose or Breath in the Afternoon,* and according to the author himself, to make it you put "One jigger of absinth into a champagne glass, add iced champagne until it attains the proper opalescent milkiness. Drink 3 to 5 slowly." His contribution got top billing, but on balance, this is just a terrible thing to do to champagne.

Still, the management at the El Floridita knew the power of celebrity endorsements. They also knew that room full of star-struck tourists getting weapons-grade on a concoction like the papa doble would be problematic. Necessity being the mother of invention, someone got creative and invented a cocktail named for Hemingway that was in the same general ballpark as the doble, but aimed at the less enthusiastic, or at least more emotionally well-adjusted, drinker.

What the barman did was swap out the cane syrup with an Italian liqueur made from maraschino cherries and add a dash of ruby red grapefruit juice. The result is so cold that is slushy, but it is *not* frozen, thus forgoing that half ounce of shame and garnish of "I deserve to be punched in the mouth" you get when consuming a frozen daiquiri in public.

Use a cocktail shaker and proper cocktail glasses, and they really are good without being so sickly sweet as the thing in tall hurricane glass you're likely to get in the wild. Hemingway himself described them as going down like a "glacier." They do, and in the oppressive heat of the South or, according to the news, Portland, Oregon, who could ask for more?

The Hemingway Daiquiri:
2 oz white rum
.75 oz lime juice
.5 oz Maraschino liqueur
.5 oz ruby red grapefruit juice
Lime wedge

Shake over cracked ice until it turns slushy. Pour into chilled cocktail glasses. Garnish with lime wedge.

Start referring to prose as "muscular" and recalling war stories you never actually witnessed.

Richard Murff

BROWN WATER

It was a hot day in Wickliffe, Kentucky, a charming little intersection of a town on the east bank of the Mississippi River. I was standing on a moored barge that housed a clever idea that was both brilliant and represented, for whisky, a great leap backward.

The Mississippi River's headwaters actually begin at Lake Itasca, in Minnesota. Its watershed (the area which drains into the river) covers 1.2 million square miles in 32 states and two Canadian Provences, or, about 40% of the continental United States. Wickliffe's, though, 660 citizens will tell you that it is the birthplace of the "Mighty Mississippi." They aren't bragging, just two miles upriver, the Mississippi and Ohio Rivers converge, and twenty miles to the east, in Paducah, the Tennessee River joins the Ohio before flowing into North America's largest artery.

The result, and you can feel it on the barge, is that there is a mind-boggling volume of water roiling underfoot. For readers unfamiliar with the Mississippi, it is not the sort of lazy river you drift down in an inner-tube. Old Man River will literally kill you.

This, I reckon, is as good a place as any to introduce Hank Ingram, founder of Brown Water Spirits, Inc., and producer of O.H. Ingram River Aged Whiskies. He is also responsible for whiskey's great leap backwards.

The nearby confluence of three powerful rivers in a world before planes, trains or automobiles did as much as anything to transform America from a rum-drinking colony to a republic of whiskey. Had the river run north from the gulf, with its access to that Caribbean sugar, things might have been different. Before the advent of steam powered paddle boats, though, traffic on the Mississippi's mighty current was decidedly one-way. Lumber companies built rafts to float the logs downriver to New Orleans, and since they were headed that way, started shipping products down river on those barge rafts, stopping at places like Memphis, spots along the (then) terrifyingly wealthy Mississippi Delta, and finally at New Orleans. Once the cargo was off-lifted, the barges were broken up and sold as lumber because there was no good way to send anything back up stream until the advent of steam-powered paddle-boats. To get home the river pilots had to travel by land.

It is straightforward to see the logistics of how river traffic brought product to market, what is less obvious is how the river traffic itself changed the product.

Vodka and gin are also made from grain, so what is it that makes whisky so different? Part of the answer is in the mash bill, or the type and proportions of grain used in the distillation The good people of Kentucky will tell you that their Commonwealth's limestone bedrock filters the water in such a way that makes it perfect for distillation. They aren't wrong, either. The fact remains, however, that whisky can be made anywhere. And all of it starts out as White Dog, White Lightning, O' Be Joyful, Kickapoo Joy-Juice or – for the sake of editorial clarity – Moonshine.

Moonshine is objectively terrible. I would know. If you'd like to know, start writing about spirits in the South for any length of time and you will collect, like the pied piper, a trail of likably bearded fellows flogging some species of moonshine for connoisseurs. They will tell you that their 'shine is some variation of Southern pride in a product that is at once traditional and next generation hep. Maybe, but that doesn't change the fact that moonshine is, again, objectively terrible. I feel obliged to be clear about this. Like wine lined with tree-resin, or the stuff made in prison toilets, in the olden days, moonshine wasn't kicked back because it was a delight, but because it was there and it got the job done. If you were going to be gentile about it, as the basic of a punch. It short, it was for people without any good choices in the matter.

Secondly, there is no such thing as next-generation moonshine because moonshine itself is a job unfinished. And not artfully so, like sushi. It's "next-generation" is a magical brown water called "whisky." The only "authenticity of craft" involved in the weird resurgence of moonshine in a market also offering great whiskies from across America, Scotland, Ireland, Japan and France is the craft of an authentically brilliant advertising professional. And that the rest of us are authentically gullible.

Maybe Kentucky water does produce a more refined moonshine, but all of it is so harsh, who can tell?* The fact is, and this is why early man was in awe of booze, what makes whiskey so wonderful is that a great deal happens in those barrels that appear to be laying around doing nothing.

In addition to the mash bill, both gin and vodka are distilled several times. Bourbon and Scotch, are distilled twice, usually, and the Irish give theirs a third go. That is why some Irish whiskies taste like Scotch with the corners sanded off. So how does that goat-piss gasoline moonshine make the jump to whisky?

This is less a matter of what is in the whisky than what the whisky is in. What makes a good whiskey is largely contact between the unfinished spirit and those charred oak staves of the whisky barrel. This caramelizes the natural sugars in the wood, which imparts a flavor and dark amber color to the whisky inside. You probably already knew that, but it does raise the question: What about the spirit in the middle if the barrel? The answer is heat cycling., and Kentucky is a good place for this, as it has cold winters and hot summers. The fluctuation causes the liquid to expand in the winter and contract in the summer, creating (very) slow movements of liquid in the barrel against those charred staves. But it doesn't move that much. The issue can be forced with climate controlled rickhouses† where you can speed up the process by artificially creating two winters and

---

* Don't you start… no you can't, either.

† A industry-wide corruption of the word "rack house" for the racks of bourbon barrels.

two summers each year. It's called heat-cycling and while purist will fuss, from the stand-point of pure physics this method works as well as what nature is already doing. It's just a little less folksy.

Another way to get the liquid moving is rolling the barrels – which is tedious, expensive and a great way to rack up OSHA lawsuits. Shaped the way they are, whiskey barrels are heavy but aren't that hard to roll, even when full. Stopping a barrel once it gets moving can be tricky for a fellow who'd like to be able to pick up his grandchild in his old age. On balance, it's cumbersome business and few distilleries take the trouble, although they don't admit it. This is a shame because rolling a barrel while the white dog slowly ages inside does a whisky a world of good.

And it was in pursuit if that concept that I found myself in a floating rickhouse with Hank Ingram in Wickliffe, Kentucky. The vessel had started life as a barge, and Hank's family had started out in the lumber trade, then went into the barge business, and now Hank is pulling it into whiskey. This makes the man something of a walking metaphor for America's whisky experience.

Hank explained the process of a whisky being aged on the humid climate of the Mississippi with river legs wobbling beneath it in the language of an involved and excited engineer, but the bottom line is this: He just lets the natural movement of the river do the sloshing for him. In Hank's defense, "sloshing" is my term. His term had more syllables.

Hank admits that the whole process is experimental, but that's the adventure. What appears to be happening is a something of dog years in whisky aging, where one year of the slow, constant movement of spirits in the barrel is equal to about three or four in a rickhouse.

He isn't the only one, Trey Zoeller over a Jefferson Distillers produces a popular Ocean series. It is interesting that the brand is named for a guy who warned against liquor but was one of the new republic's first really high-profile wine snob – Thomas Jefferson.

Before America could make decent wine the upper class was crazy about a fortified wine called Madeira, made on the eponymous island off the coast of Spain. It was Madeira, not bourbon or rum, that was used to toast the signing of the Declaration of Independence. Its producers had long known to fortify the wine with grape spirits and then sent it back and forth the equator no fewer than four times for the good stuff. This is exactly what the man's namesake distiller is doing. Modern ocean going vessels being the way they are, there isn't a lot of "sloshing." Those Jefferson Ocean barrels crossing the equator four times, will benefit from steady heat exchange and the salt air.

Innovations, however clever, are only as good as their results. Both whiskies are fantastic.

In the Ingram floating rickhouse, we sampled a couple of whiskies out of the cask. They were very good, and seemed to me well-worth the effort. I've never actually gotten into "cask strength" expressions that are so trendy these days. Despite what the deranged whisky enthusiast will tell you – the human tongue just can't process the nuances of anything at that proof. It's not a matter of a discerning palate, it's just physics. If the goal is just to get legless, sure, knock it back. As far as *tasting* the stuff is concerned, your system will just be too overwhelmed to pick up those "vanilla notes" you're trying to get everyone in the room to believe that you're tasting.

The other reason for not delving too deep into the cask strength craze was reduced to a very sensible formula by that bourbon fan Walker Percy in his essay for *Esquire* magazine, sensibly titled "Bourbon":

> If one derives the same pleasure from knocking back 80-proof Bourbon as 100-proof, the formula is both as simple as $2+2 = 4$ and as incredible as non-Euclidean geometry. Consider. One knocks back five one ounce shots of 80-proof Early Times or four shots of 100-proof Old Fitzgerald. The alcohol ingestion is the same:
> $$5 \times 40\% = 2$$
> $$4 \times 50\% = 2$$
> Yet, in the case of Early Times, one has obtained an extra quantum of joy without cost to the liver, brain, or gastric mucosa. A bonus, pure and simple, and an aesthetic gain as incredible as two parallel lines meeting at infinity.

Don't roll your eyes, Walker Percy was a medical doctor. Although he contracted tuberculosis as an intern and never practiced. While recuperating, be read a great deal. Rather too much you might argue, because after that he became something of a philosopher. It shows.

As fun as it is to drink well-made whisky out of the cask while the long-suffering Mrs. M's hair re-curls in direct defiance to her hair-straightener, I prefer it in the bottle. In the bottle, Ingram is one of those whiskies that goes well with a little water or a single cube of ice, which dissipates any heat (not much to speak of) and leaves an almost creamy feel.

The spice will lend to an excellent Old Fashioned if you don't like them too sweet. Hank wouldn't tell me exactly how old it was, and it's not on the bottle, but I suppose that's the point. The rules of *terra firma* don't really apply here. It tastes like it's spent all the time it jolly-well needs in the barrel, and beyond that, you really shouldn't care too much.

A Sense of Place

I started this chapter on brown water at a specific geographic locale, rather than a point in time or a boozy cultural exchange, because whisky, more than any other spirit seems to evoke a sense of place. Rum may be a lifestyle choice, but whisky is a point on the map. More often than not, a place with roots.

So much so that while the spellings *Whisky* and *Whiskey* are both correct and can be used interchangeably, in practice how the word is spelled depends on a sense of place. Ireland and America use the superfluous "E", which is dispensed with in Scotland and Canada. Even this convention isn't applied hard and fast, Old Forester and Maker's Mark both drop the "E", and they nothing if not American.

After that, things tend to get more pedantic. Scotch whisky can only be made in Scotland – not England, not Wales. Bourbon doesn't have to be made in Kentucky (but about 95% if it is) but it must be produced in the United States. Canadian whisky is called just that. Japanese distillers have taken the trouble to dismantle entire distilleries in Scotland and rebuild them in Japan, some have even imported all the ingredients (including the water) but it isn't Scotch. It's Japanese whisky, and runs along the palette as a

```

lighter Lowland Scotch and includes local ingredients like lemongrass in the bill. Some of it is fantastic. So much so that Dewar's now offers an expression finished in Japanese mizunara oak casks called appropriately enough *Japanese Smooth*.

The French are starting to make the stuff and even the Nordic countries are getting into the act with some impressive results. And the world's number one producer of whisky is…India. Although good luck finding a bottle of the stuff off the subcontinent, they don't export it. With good reason, I understand.

Although I hear it fairly often, the distinction between bourbon and Tennessee whiskey is not due to some Hatfield-McCoy type hillbilly feud between the states. As much fun as that would be, it is really a matter of process.

A few years ago, I called Jeff Arnett, then the master distiller at the Jack Daniel Distillery. As he explained, to call a whisky "bourbon" requires it to go through a very specific process: at least 51% of the mash bill must be corn, but no more than 79% (at 80% it becomes corn whiskey). How much barley, wheat and rye a distiller uses fluctuates. Then it needs to be laid up in new charred, white oak barrels.*

Tennessee whiskey follows the same process as bourbon before going rogue on its final step, whereupon its mellowed

---

* Afterward, the used barrels are mostly sold to Scotch distillers who use them a couple of times more.
```

through ten feet of sugar maple charcoal. In the words of Arnett "We do bourbon one better."

Exactly how did Jack Daniel stumble on to this final innovation? He didn't. The credit for that goes to the man who would become the distillery's first head distiller, Nathan Green. Although everyone who ever met the man called him Uncle Nearest. Don't ask me why.

Uncle Nearest was the slave of, and Jack the chore-boy for, a Lutheran preacher named Call. Durning the week, Call had a farm and a very well regarded whisky still that had gained some local fame.

Remember all that trouble ancient societies has in finding clean drinking water after they stopped roaming? And if you've been reading very closely you'll recall a fun fact on page 45 involving a method for cleaning funky water with charcoal filters. Medieval Europeans seemed to have forgotten the trick, but it clung on in Africa and is one of those traditional things brought over from the old country and passed down during slavery. I couldn't tell you why the man applied the technique to whisky which had already been distilled, but he did and it added a mellow sweetness to the final product.

Perhaps the Rev. Call, or more likely Mrs. Call, thought that the whisky business wasn't setting the proper tone for his righteous flock. Call sold the still to a 13 year old Jack. To modern eyes, giving a whisky still to a well-armed teenager would seem a short-sighted thing to do, but there is a lot about this story that doesn't sit well. As it turns out, young Jack Daniel was no ordinary boy with the capacity for industrial whisky production. If nothing else, he was smart enough to know who actually knew how make the stuff.

By 1866, the Jack Daniel Distillery was licensed and running. It employed America's first black head distiller, Uncle Nearest Green. That much we know,. Exactly what the Old No. 7 means is lost to us. Even Jeff Arnett didn't know.* Was the recipe the seventh attempt? Did the J in his signature look like a seven? One popular legend has it that young Jack had seven girlfriends at the time and wanted to dedicate his whisky to them all. Anything is possible and to this day that whisky is helping young and old alike get lucky in love.

What we do know is that in 1910, Jack made the tragic mistake of going into the office early. Unable to remember the combination of the office safe at that unsocial hour, he kicked the safe and broke his toe. The subsequent infection killed him.

And yet his Tennessee whiskey still snakes through the sugar-maple charcoals to this day and can't, for that reason, be called bourbon.

It's not the only one either.

More recently the Nearest Green distillery has been established and produces under the Uncle Nearest label. You've probably had Jack Daniel's before. Uncle Nearest, maybe not. It's worth picking up a bottle, it's a brilliant Tennessee Whisky.

---

* Or he wouldn't tell me.

Richard Murff

Kentucky, USA

I was sitting with some friends in a basement bar under Louisville's famed Whiskey Row sipping from a $230 bottle of 23-year-old bourbon. It was a dark, wood paneled place somewhere under the Evan Williams building and it would have been a thing of beauty but for the feel of being on a movie set. Still the whisky was something to sing about and, of course, we were singing the usual foolishness about caramel notes, heat, hints of vanilla and pouty insolence.

My grandfather drank Evan Williams and I had the vague notion, even as a kid, that it wasn't particularly fine. Nobody's grandfather drank particularly fine bourbon for the simple reason that there wasn't any particularly fine bourbon to be had in their day. There was plenty of *good* bourbon, but no one what carrying on about the stuff. Even when a writer of Walker Percy's caliber leans into the subject and he starts in on non-Euclidean geometry. What we were drinking under Whiskey Row that afternoon was definitely not the brown water I snuck out of my parent's liquor cabinet.

This is what a guy's road trip looks like on the far side of forty: A little calmer, the bars a little cleaner and the drinks a lot better. All of which made me feel very sophisticated until

I looked at my watch and noted that almost exactly twenty-four hours earlier, after a well lubricated lunch in Nashville, there had been car-to-car mooning. As it turns out, being a fourteen-year-old boy is a little like herpes: It's controllable but there is no known cure. While a boy can walk out the door and "play" for twelve hours without needing to explain himself, after a certain age it's considered bad form not to have a plan.

One of the gang told his wife "We are all just students of the craft." Which is why he's in sales and I sit around writing waggish histories. His wife is some species of financial mastermind who was kind enough not to laugh out loud at us.

Bourbon, in Kentucky at least, is no laughing matter. It has caused the small hamlet of Bardstown too morph to a destination which CNN ranked in the "Top Ten All American Experiences." The distiller's association's Kentucky Bourbon Trail now draws more than a million people annually. Which is great for business except for the persistent rumor that the Bourbon Capital of the World is running out of the stuff.

That "student of the craft" bit wasn't pure bullshit… just about 75% pure. Which isn't bad considering that on any given day the industry itself believes 90% of its own BS. That's because (and this should be obvious by now) that the industry doesn't really know how it got where it currently happens to be. The whole whisky story, like the confluence of rivers sloshing Hank Ingram's barrels so artfully, is itself a confluence of happy accidents, false starts, reverse engineering and bald market opportunism. None of which producers like to admit to customers.

At the Heaven Hill Bourbon Heritage Center in Bardstown, they'll tell you that one Elijah Craig, preacher and distiller (because, evidently ye olde Protestant God used to be pretty mellow on the booze question), suffered a fire in his warehouse. The constraints of the physical universe be damned, the blaze only charred only the *inside* of the barrels. Being too cheap to replace said barrels, Rev. Craig accidentally invented modern bourbon.

Meanwhile, down in the basement of the Evans Williams building (also owned by Heaven Hill) the fellow in a prohibition era straw boater told me how the same righteous tightwad, Rev. Craig, bought some second-hand barrels that had been previously used to transport salted fish, so he charred the insides to remove the fishy taste. I don't know much, but I know enough to fact check a man wearing a boater in this day and age. I might also suggest that the good people in the Heaven Hill marketing department get their story straight.

I called Chris Morris, the master distiller at Brown-Forman responsible for Old Forester and Woodford Reserve. Chris knows bourbon, it's the only job he's ever had. His father worked for the company and was the first employee to jump from hourly to management. One summer when Chris was 16, his father told him that the master distiller needed some help, so go make himself useful. Chris did as he was told and ended up working summers for the distillery throughout college, and has been there ever since. He's also a member of Louisville's Filson Historical Society and a serious amateur historian. I mean amateur in the British sense that he's devoted to the science or art, *not* that he isn't good enough to go pro. He is. A guy that stable can only be only about 1.5-2% full of it. Which is all you can ask of a functioning adult these days.

"First of all," Chris said as we drove around Louisville, "you can't make a barrel *without* heating the staves. That's the only way to get the wood to bend." Every barrel ever constructed of wooden staves since the beginning of barrel-making has its insides heated and for most of human history that involved an open flame. That no one overdid it is a hard sell. Secondly, the ancient Phoenicians charred barrels on purpose as water filters.

Then there is also the implausible theory that Rev. Craig was trying to get the fish smell out of the barrels. "Yes, people reused barrels," Chris told me with a hint of exasperation at the persistence of the story, "but people reused barrels for the same purpose. They wouldn't have stored whisky in a barrel made for fish any more than we'd use an iPhone as a microwave."

The story isn't quirky enough for a man in a boater, but this business of using whisky as a store of wealth probably had something to do with it. The stuff was starting to get laid up for a long time. The benefits of time spent in a barrel for taste was nothing new. Really, people had been laying up booze since about the sixth century.

Add in the odd and accidental over-charred barrel and the whisky began to change and mellow as the temperature fluctuations drew the liquor in and out of the wood. Once you loaded it on barged to head down river, all that sloshing just speeded up the process.

"They used to call it red whisky," Chris told me. With its deeper, smoother flavor, it proved popular. With a little if the same reverse engineering and trial and error humans have been up to since Chapter One, distillers where able to sort out the trick of forcing something that was already happening naturally.

Which brings us back to that confluence of the Ohio, Tennessee and Mississippi rivers. America is a melting pot, and the first big market for that "red whisky" probably wasn't Kentucky at all, but New Orleans.

As the Mississippi River opened up to American traders, Louisiana still wanted to be French. The whisky that was shipped down to New Orleans marked "Bourbon County" and sat in barrels longer and mimicked the colors, flavors and feel of the Creole's beloved cognac, but at a fraction of the price. The new style spread.

Bourbon became the all-American Spirit, more or less, by trying to impress the French.

PROHIBITION

It is good advice: Beware the absolute "shall."
Society needs a little wiggle room and absolutes
rarely achieve their stated goals. Because
humans are essentially ambitious morons, making something
taboo is a great way to make people want it more. The
Qu'ran forbids intoxicating drinks and suddenly everyone is
reading *Khamriyat* poetry – that randy genre of "Fear and
Loathing in the Non-Muslim Quarter" of the medieval Arab
world.* Or the glamour of America's prohibition that is so
ingrained in the national psyche that Evan Williams is still
celebrating whisky as contraband with a tasting room that
looks like a speak-easy. Before we get to prohibition, though,
the drinking had to get out of hand.

T'was Thomas Jefferson who wrote "Good wine is a
necessity of life for me." He also thought that hard
liquor was going to spell ruin for the republic.

Well, not quite. This wasn't a matter of Jefferson being
an alarmist, but Americans of his day hadn't quite got the

---

* I was in Libya at the start of their civil war and can assure you
that the place is lousy with homemade liquor.

social handle around the hard stuff, which was made even more difficult in areas that were laughably isolated from the sort of social pressures that tends to keep all but the most lively drinker (somewhat) in-line. In London society had gotten so big that you could just disappear in the mob. In America, however, was so wide-open, that you could just disappear, period.

As a consequence, by the 19th century Americans went around gassed all the damn time. Frontier towns were pretty rough places, and it showed in the saloon and, in the larger cities, the bar. Women didn't set foot in them. Whether this was men being oppressive or women taking one look at the place and saying, "I don't think so!" is hard to say.

At any rate, the saloon would be conveniently located between a fellow's place of employment and the house. This caused a problem for the Mrs., as she was likely to be a real wet sandwich about his drinking the hard-earned money rather that spending it on things like food for the children and rent. You can't blame her. After all, she'd spent 40 weeks carrying the little stinkers while they made outrageous caloric and territorial demands on *her*. Like hell was she going to let them die of starvation or exposure because her husband wanted to drink the paycheck. This, the ladies found vexing. One vexed lady is one thing, but when the entire tribe gets worked up they are likely to pull out the 19th century version of a *#metoo* movement. Which, in this case, was prohibition.

The somewhat obviously titled novel *Ten Nights in a Bar-Room and What I Saw There* was the second best selling novel of its day after *Uncle Tom's Cabin*. The novel presents a dreadful world of saloon keepers as the crack dealers of their day, praying on otherwise hardworking, God-fearing family men to fill them to the gills with demon rum, corn liquor and red whisky in order to suck up the family's money and leave them all in poverty. So strong was the hold drink had on these fallen men that the little girl coming into the place to beg daddy to come home to his loving, but destitute, family couldn't even penetrate his pickled heart. Booze-fueled tragedy is heaped upon booze-fueled tragedy until dad is dead and mom and the kids, beaten senseless by life, are now homeless in the bargain. The book, on balance, was a real downer.

How rampant all these grim scenarios actually were is debatable. Popular novels, like social media, are not very good reflections of what is actually going on in a society. They are, however, very good reflections of what people *imagine* is going on. The book did strick a hell of a chord across the country. While records are notoriously spotty we might make a reasonable guess that even if *Ten Nights* is a theatrical exaggeration, there was a real underlying and pervasive problem there to be exaggerated.

The first tremors of the prohibition movement in American wasn't really anti-alcohol, but anti-saloon. These women had no problem with, say, some Italian *nona* taking a nip of chianti while she made a cauldron of *sauce* for eight children, their spouses and 47 grandchildren. Nor was it some well-heeled titan of industry and his socialite wife having a glass of sherry after dinner to celebrate the university library they'd just funded that caused offense. The German *beirgarten* was actually considered wholesome, filled as it was with men, women and children. The latter of whom act as an effective hedge against getting completely blotto as there ever was. It wasn't until 1914, when we went to war with Germany that carrying on about the Fatherland and beer got decidedly unfashionable and not at all wholesome.

What the prohibition movement stood against was what this generation would call the "toxic masculinity" of the saloon. And in that original sense prohibition actually worked.

Some political movements are about the individual or collective rights of a certain groups. The other relevant feminist movement of the time , women's suffrage, leaps to mind. In women gaining the right to vote, men didn't lose anything. Then there are coercive political movements which demand that one group impose its will on another, say the "drys" against the "wets." And this being America, a third group arose, the "drinking drys" who drank themselves but thought other shouldn't.

Any coercive type of political movement needs political allies because people, certainly Americans, don't like being bossed around. The feminist Anti-Saloon League (ASL) was no different. What really gave the movement its boost was an alliance with the suffrage movement. The female vote was coming and most politicians knew that the prohibition was its sister movement. So to woo the approaching ladies' vote, you had to court the ASL.

What was less clear was what, exactly, was being prohibited. Politicians, being politicians, passed the 18th Amendment banning "intoxicating" drinks without ever defining just what that meant. Beer brewers and wine vintners assumed that the law didn't apply to them.

As often happens in movements with reasonable aims, they get hijacked by the most radical members. The aims of the original ASL might have be summed up as: *Jesus, fellas, just pump the brakes on the hard stuff! Look, honey, I don't mean to snap, I really don't. I know that you work hard all day in the factory, and you want to relax before coming home and pumping me full of a dozen children... but remember that the washing machine, dryer, dishwasher, vacuum cleaner, take-out restaurants or modern child-care haven't been invented yet. And when they are, I still won't think that cleaning up after you is all that fun, you Neanderthal. Grocery shopping done in dinky crates and wagons scattered across three city-blocks. Give it a century, honey, and huge corporations will charge through the nose to all this quaint inconvenience, but right now it's just tedious. And useless without the money you're spending on putting the local barkeep's kids through college. That kid will be a senator one day. Meanwhile jr. has rickets and I'd like to go out and get all girl-drink drunk with my friends too, you know. So... knock it off, Buster, my life isn't a box of bon-bons either.*

Or word to that affect.

The second wave of the movement took things a bit further with an absolute shall not, and drafted a memo of complete abstinence, nothing over .5% ABV, and handed it to one Andrew Volstead to put before a congress looking down the barrel of the women's vote.

The American experiment wasn't the first time in history that society took a long look at itself and decided that it needed to dry out. While China doesn't leave as much physical evidence as the arid Middle East for the drinking historian, what there is pretty ancient. What you really get in China, once writing was introduced around 1,200 BC, is heaps of laws banning the sauce.

Considered the first Chinese Empire, the Han dynasty, was the most technologically advanced in the world at the time. They didn't invent writing, but they invented paper. After that, China's (long) history of laws and attempts at social control over its population gets a lot easier to follow. It became one of the few societies to develop at least part of their national identity around a rich *bureaucratic* tradition. Usually, a bureaucracy is a treated like a tedious necessity useful in keeping society's wheels on the gravel. Not China.

The other society that seemed to wrap itself around a bureaucracy rather that the other way around were the Ottomans. It is worth noting that both issued very literate decrees against tying one on. The end result being heaps of historical evidence pointing to cultures that a) didn't drink much and b) had stacks of laws outlawing drinking so damn much.

How successful were these prohibition laws? Presumably not very, or the bureaucrats wouldn't have kept passing all those laws. In their defense though, the weight of cultural history and evolution was stacked against them.

The earliest examples of prohibition pre-date writing, so you get lots of legends passed along orally for a few thousand years. As anyone who has ever sent a child to deliver a message to his wife knows, the mutations in communication can get pretty wide with just one messenger over say, 45 seconds. For historical purposes, these drinking tales morphing over 10 generations are fairly useless, but not entirely. Persistent tales, true or not, hold some social value in their mere persistence. The lies people come up will often tell you more about them than the truth.

There is not one, but two, legends of bad Chinese emperors with horrible concubines building a lake of wine to paddle around in to quaff the stuff while naked nymphos and toyboys swim around and have orgies.* Once the novelty of the Wino Fun Park wears off, the nasty wife or concubine orders a thousand men to drain the lake by drinking it dry, and laughs hysterically when they all drown.

There is something "Adam & Eve" about these stories: Sure, both are pretty awful, but it's always the gal who is just a little *more* awful. This is less than fair. Besides, he was the emperor.

At any rate, both stories end with the emperor being overthrown and his entire dynasty brought to ruin through drink and a regrettable woman. Di Xin, the last emperor of the Shang Dynasty was real, but the lake o' wine tale ought to be filed alongside George Washington's cherry tree. We really don't know who came up with the story, other than it was probably a guy who was likely scared of the Mrs. It's just one of those cautionary tales about drinking that have been cropping us since the beginning of time; like Dionysus turning a boat-load of bi-curious sailors into dolphins.

The semi-regular bans on alcohol, though, were rarely absolute. Drinking was relegated to formal occasions like marriage, funeral and temple rites. After the authorities started writing everything down, there is no shortage of

* Emperor Jie (1,728-1,675 BC supposedly) and Di Xin the last Emperor of the Shang Dynasty – making a first-hand account just barely plausible.

ancient complaints about people gate-crashing the funerals of anyone without a pulse to get their hands on a snort.

What we seeing here is some pretty solid patterns in the relationship between humanity, civilization and cocktail hour. As a bonding exercise it causes you to let your guard down with the group, which is good for the pack. Up to a point. It's also something to get a bit wary of. If you don't want the whole pack to lose its head, you need to have some ground rules. You don't need to get all Spartan about it, but going full tilt Puss & Mew seems ill-advised as well. Yes, the drink makes you feel warm and fuzzy and tall and good looking. It makes a grim reality less so. This was where the (sometime tedious) invention of old people comes in handy: Somebody has to tell you to knock it off.

By the first century BC, Chinese traders were trading regularly with boozy Mesopotamia and the horn of Africa. Like anyplace else, China suffered its invasions, civil wars and the odd cyclical golden age. The second was the Ming Dynasty (1368-1644), and Silk Road trade, what we might call an early globalization, had the place booming. Shipping of exotic alcohol would have been impractical, but the exchange in technology and ingredients would have been astounding. Sadly, it all came to a screeching halt with the fall of the Ming's and establishment of China's last dynasty, the Qing (1644-1912) which enacted an isolationist policy in order to combat Japanese piracy. The policy didn't do much to stop the pirates, but it absolutely cratered the economy for almost three centuries where the society simply regressed.

I point this out, not to digress into economics, but this mismanagement did affect Asian drinking culture. First, that former powerhouse of China became weak and inward looking at the same time the Europeans started sniffing around for place to loot. Second, while it did little to stop the pirates* but it did lay the ground work for the opium trade.

Unlike booze, which had been socialized over a couple of millennia with several attempts to put a lid on things the opium trade really put the zap on a culture. You can see the effects even today. You haven't lived until you drink cobra blood in Hong Kong.

By the time that Capitol Hill passed the 18th Amendment, nearly half of Americans already lived under some form of state prohibition. And it wasn't just we in the land of puritanical hypocrisy either: Finland enacted prohibition that same year and New Zealand very nearly did until the absentee ballots of the soldiers overseas came in. Russia, of all places, was five years into the vodka ban enacted by Tzar Nicholas II. Nicholas had enacted the ban in 1914, which was short sighted because about a quarter of the state revenue came from taxes on vodka sales, and you do not want to take a pay cut like that on the run up to a very expensive World War. At it was, four years later a grateful proletariat murdered the old guy and his entire family for good measure. Iceland was next with a booze ban in 1915 and then Norway in 1917.

So America's noble experiment, may have been "noble" but it wasn't terribly "experimental." It is also a myth that

---

* Honestly, if they were interested in what was legal they wouldn't have been pirates?

alcohol consumption went up overall during prohibition. In most of the country evidence points to alcohol consumption dropping off, not to zero, but in that direction. Most of the country, though, was rural: Far away from big city organized crime and too sparsely populated to make it worth the trip.

Yes, there were heaps of backwoods stills serving the rural market. Given the great distances involved, they invented a lively distribution system that utilized wild-eyed hillbillies drive hell for leather all over the place to avoid the law. Sound like fun.? You bet it does! These guys had so much fun doing it that when prohibition was repealed they invented NASCAR to keep doing it. Even then, though, there was still an "everyone knows your momma" element of rural society that depressed demand. The women of the Methodist Ladies Auxiliary were still pretty worked up about the saloon.

The major cities were a different matter. Before she died at the age of 101, my grandmother on the Jaubert side swore without a hint of irony or even humor that, I'm quoting here, "New Orleans never had prohibition." Well, legally speaking, she was wrong, but culturally, she dead right.

New Orleans didn't take to the yankee handover with much more grace than the Spanish one. There is a Jaubert family tale about Gran's older sister (she was youngest of ten) who caught hell from their dad for going out with a boy who didn't speak French. Being a predominately Mediterranean, Catholic culture, New Orleans just ignored the whole prohibition business and the whole prohibition business, by and large, just ignored New Orleans.

Big cities like New York and Chicago, on the other hand, went nuts like freshmen undergrads. There were a lot of speak-easies that probably looked like the thing you're currently imagining: Jazz, blacks and whites drinking together for the first time in ever, Scott and Zelda Fitzgerald making themselves obvious, Bill Faulkner wandering around pantsless for the weekend. And the flapper. Ironically, it is this femininely tipsy gal who became he embodiment of prohibition's success, not its failure. We'll get back to her in a bit.

Most "speak-easies" were just rooms in boarding houses. More to the point, Italian boarding houses, where you could come and have a glass of wine with your pasta. Food historians cite prohibition the point where American first got its taste for Italian food. Why Italians? Well, with a lot of Italians in the police force, it was easy for the aforementioned smiling *nona* having a glass of chianti with her sauce to be "overlooked" by law enforcement.* Who the hell is going to arrest their *nona*? Which raises the other question: In a country with national prohibition and no wine industry, where were they getting the wine? Basically, it was flowing in between the separation of church and state.

Here we have one of the *plus ça change* examples of civilization. Like the Chinese exempting temple rites and funerals from prohibition, the Catholic church was exempted from the Volstead act in its use of sacramental wine. It could legally buy wine for sacramental purposes from American

---

* You could say the say thing about the Irish, but Irish food is terrible.

wineries. Enough that grape production in California alone went up by 700%. *Very strictly speaking*, the church probably didn't sell *much* sacramental wine to parishioners, although, I'd imagine donations went up miraculously.*

A 1925 report from the Federal Council of Churches of Christ reported that nearly three million gallons of wine had been claimed for sacramental use during the first two years of prohibition. The report concluded, "There is no way of knowing what the legitimate consumption of fermented sacramental wine is, but it is clear that the legitimate demand does not increase 800,000 gallons in two years."

Well, no, probably not.

The amount of sacramental wine used by the America's Catholic churches stayed at those comically inflated levels until the 18ᵗʰ Amendment was repealed 13 years later. Whereupon it dropped, almost immediately, to pre-prohibition levels.

One unintended effect of shutting down the saloons was the invention of the modern bar. When the saloons went away, something else stepped into the cirrhosis vacuum. New, and completely illegal, there weren't any old rules governing the speak-easy. There was no precedent to say that women couldn't drink there as well. So they did.

Remember back when I mentioned that the first Roman Bacchanalia was a girl-night out and no one really thought too much about it until the fellas got involved and it went to

* The rumor was that when William Faulkner lived in New Orleans, across an alley from St. Louis Cathedral, his bootlegger was a priest.

hell? You could argue that the ladies barging their way in the American bar-room had the same effect, in reverse. The year after prohibition was repealed alcohol consumption had fallen to half the level of the pre-prohibition years.

Let's be clear about women and their drinking habits: The evidence doesn't support that they are fundamentally more sensible than the guys. I'm sure that they think that they are, but don't we all? I'd invite any one who doesn't believe this to spend a weekend in Nashville, Tennessee – currently the nation's top destination for bachelorette parties. Specifically, the Broadway entertainment district where the theatrical bacchanal is entertaining as hell.

As dusk settles, they will emerge from hotels rooms: Swarms of drunken gals in short shorts or cocktail dresses with cowboy boots riding electric scooters that flit in and out of the congested Music City traffic. They travel in packs which will consist of one lady in a tiara and sash, drinking some weapons-grade hooch from a water bottle that looks like a 24-fluid ounce boner. She's madly in love with someone in another state. The rest of the swarm, her lifelong BFFs, will be wearing rhinestone studded cowboy hats. They'll be madly jealous, which explains why they are forcing bride to drink a Moscow Mule out of a huge penis. Together these young women will make more noise than all the country acts blasting from the rooftop bars for three city blocks.

My twin brother is a doctor in Nashville and he asked a friend who works in a local emergency room about the phenomenon. In describing the sheer number of head traumas that come in every weekend from these parties he said, "It's a bloodbath."

All of which to say that women, on their own, aren't really any better at drinking than men. My theory is that our drinking habits tend to go gonzo when drinking within a group with whom you feel comfortable and *the option of sex is off the table*. Men and women drink together under the social threat of looking like an ass in front of your date, which is enough to keep things generally in proportion. At least until the orgy starts. (See Hathor.)

I n the end, prohibition was not repealed because people thought that it was a bad idea, but as an economic stimulus in the first years of the depression. People needed jobs and the dread saloon had more or less gone away.

Another added benefit of prohibition was improved race relations. The police in large cities at the time didn't really do much "policing" of black neighborhoods. There primary objective was, more or less, to keep blacks in their own neighborhood where they'd sort out their issues without disturbing the white people, or the rich ones at any rate. The practical affect being that to open a speak-easy in a white part of town, you had to grease a lot of palms. In black parts of town, fewer people were looking, so whites went *there* to drink to escape from the laws that they'd passed because they were scared of their wives. And then invited their wives.

So it was that men, women, blacks and whites sat down together for the first time in the Republic's tortured history and had a decent drink.

Drunk as Lords

And it might be time to do it again.

Epilogue:

The Hangover and Why that's Useful living

The main drawback to a really dramatic hangover is that all that is awaiting you, should you pull through, is sobriety; something better left in the past or the future, but overrated in the present. Amateurs will say that hangovers are to be avoided because of the pain involved. You and I know better; the pain, according to those methodical Germans, only makes us stronger. Grouchy, but stronger.

Pain suffers a double standard. If following something that's fun, it's considered unhealthy. While pain that follows something that isn't fun, like lifting an iron bar over your head, or running three miles when you've got a perfectly good, is healthy. Damn Puritans.

A hangover gives you hope. It gives you something to look forward to, and if you're one of those who absolutely must put a negative spin on it, and hangover gives you something to avoid. A hangover can be educational: Think of the experimental chemistry tried in the name of finding a cure for last night's experimental chemistry. P.G. Wodehouse's Jeeves had a famed hangover cure of a raw egg, Worcestershire and Tabasco - sometimes brandy. This is a potent combination and if combined with caffeine, soda water, aspirin, and a long nap will certainly do the trick. If you haven't got that much time, playing basketball in the 90 degree sun until you throw up will put you right as rain.

These days you can find something called a hangover patch: It might help you hydrate with a pain killers, but it will do nothing for the grim hours of depressed introspection that awaits you.

Before you go invest in some old world or high tech hangover cure, consider the following. It's a Wednesday Night and you only want to have a beer with some pals and shoot some pool or eat something your wife won't allow in the house. So what do you do? You go find a bar with a television. Fine. Then you and the gang find a place that is beautiful in its darkness and foul aroma. There should be anywhere from three to 57 screens and not one of them tuned to the Lifetime network.

As luck would have it, ESPN12 isn't showing the score of the Australian Rules football game and you can't go home until you know if the North Melbourne Kangaroos are going to pull through. So you stay for another round, just until they show the score and the announcers make some commentary because none of you know the rules to Australian Rules football. You can forgive the fact that it looks like they're playing rugby because the injuries are so graphic.

The Roos score and one of the announcers says they've almost closed the gap. Well, you've got to see if they close the gap. You've got too. Then that little voice pipes up. It's Wednesday night, if you don't get yourself to the bed you're gonna feel like hell tomorrow. Gluttony is not the issue here, acting like a real ass certainly isn't either. The threat of having to go to work with a hairy hangover is the only thing keeping you from ordering a round of shots on a Wednesday night. This, of course, is exactly what you do when the Roos score and take the lead. Good on ya' Mate.

Damn those shots are rough, and they smell too, better get another beer so you don't reek of liquor when you go home. The voice is still there, "You're gonna feel like hell!" This isn't the voice of common sense, that's what the non-drinkers will tell you but don't believe them. It's the voice of hard won experience.

There is another voice now. It's your friendly bartender, we'll call him Stan. Stan is offering you another drink every ten minutes because you've started to over-tip. He's a good guy, a working man. He needs the money or he wouldn't be serving you beer on a Wednesday night. Have one more round, for Stan. You all toast Stan and over-tip again. You get another round of shots, on the house. Good ole Stan. Gotta wash that liquor smell off your breath.

Whoever the hell the Kangaroos are playing just scored. Who are they? The Blues? What the hell, it's no stranger than the Crimson Tide! So what's the score now? Damn foreigners shouldn't play some strange game and call it football, it's confusing. Your beer is nearly empty and the little voice tells you again that you're gonna feel like rot, but all is not lost because now is the time to make a graceful exit and avoid further damage.

Aahhhah….You're in a meaningful conversation now. This is male bonding, the very reason you fellas got together in the first place. More than that, this is a connection to the eternal: The Greek symposium for modern life. Although, the tree sap and saltwater in your wine is a bit much. You talk about how those damned ex-convicts down under don't know how to play football. They can drink some rum, though. And who in the hell is that dude in the lab coat? Is he a doctor? Cause he's acting like a ref. And what's with the flags? There aren't any cars around… or are they? This could get interesting. You wonder if this is a championship game. Is Carlton up for a three-peat like the Chicago all those years ago? Remember Michael Jordan?

Of course you remember Michael Jordan….

Now you're thinking about Chicago. Nothing goes together like some rugby-lookin' sport and the Windy City. The best part about driving to Chicago is that from downtown Memphis, you're halfway there. Well, if you're originally from New Orleans you're halfway there. Another round of shots to celebrate the impending trip to Louisiana, then another round of beer to wash away that liquor smell. Not that New Orleans doesn't tolerate liquor on your breath, but that little voice in your head is now doing a very convincing impression of your wife, or some other life harnessing entity, let's call it Bill's stomach.

Bill just vomited between his legs under the bar. Good ole Stan loses that easy going air. He seems to have places to go suddenly. You yell at Bill, all of you do. It's to show Stan you don't approve of that sort of thing, but then you notice the Aussie football is no longer being shown. Stan, it appears, has turned it to the Lifetime network and is mopping up the bar. Banishment, and its Bill's fault, you tell him so.

Now that you're outside and moving towards your car, looking at the vehicle that will deliver you on beer-fueled monkeyshines in Chicago or New Orleans or where ever you were going, the idea doesn't seem so hot. The road trip falls through, you all blame it on Bill. This is where the utility of the hangover really shows.

Without a hangover, the cold shoulder you get at home would be a mystery. Without the hangover, those useless hours the next day you spend in the office before taking a two-hour lunch would be in vain. With the hangover you reminisce and consider your performance from the night before. Think of it like football players watching game films on Monday afternoon. You consider what you did wrong; consider what caused the condition you're now suffering (because we all know that a hangover is caused by one particular drink, not a combination of the sum). You become a better drinker.

Plato said so. Or was it Socrates? Hell, look it up, it's in Chapter Three… Or is it Four? Geez Murff, chapter numbers would have helped. You say as much at Becky from accounting who's been making judgey comments all morning. She doesn't think you are a philosopher, but won;t rule out a stroke carrying on like that.

Either way, you've changed the subject. And Becky can go to hell because you've seen the Instagram feed from Nashville.

If you're Bill, and can't remember anything after the first quarter of the polo match you were watching the night before, there is no better vehicle than a mind-splitting headache and an ever present, stomach churning bile taste on your tongue to tell you that a good time was had by all. It's certainly less humiliating than the fact that your phone is about to start ringing off the hook with varying accounts of your performance. And, Bill, by five o'clock all your confederates will be trying to convince you that you kissed that barfly who looks like Becky from Accounting. Don't you believe them. You be you Bill, you be you.

If you're not Bill, everyone except Becky has commented on how quiet you were today. No killing time in the break room for you, no sir, you were killing time at your desk, the way you're supposed to. You were *reflecting*.

Reflection is good. In this age of road rage, air rage, #hashtagrage and being forced to listen to the moral arrogance of the political left and right, doesn't it stand to reason that a little time for reflection is in order? The Zen Buddhists are lousy with reflection. Sure deadlines have slipped, but you, gentle reader, have gotten to know yourself a little better.

On the drive home, your condition is improving. Your wife will be less annoyed with you, probably even amused by now if you didn't keep her up all night begging for sex. Then a car cuts you off, more than that, bisects three lanes of traffic to cut you off and then slows down like an old man in a hat. What do you do? Flip him off, start something, show him who, exactly, is boss? No, you weep silently to yourself about the humanity of it all: Violent climax avoided and the world is just a little more peaceful.

All because you had time to reflect, and if not reflection, it takes time to sort out your thoughts if they're coming to you in Esperanto. No rash decisions for you. Even if your feeble mind did produce an off-the-cuff thought, you wouldn't know what it was for five minutes.

What's more, if you can't hold down solid foods weight loss is a snap. Keep that youthful shape by drinking like a youth. Have you ever wondered why your company is always looking for that fresh spirit? God knows it's not because they have any more to offer beyond limitless energy and a willingness to do another's bidding for a while. It's no secret that about the time you start leading a decent life, youth outruns you. Although there is a certain justified arrogance at becoming fat and not caring one way or the other, the powers that be do start looking elsewhere for the youthful vision they, as well as you, have lost. They have fresh ideas because they have time to reflect.

While on the subject of youth, don't trust those go-getters from "elite" schools who don't drink in order to "remain on the top of their game." They've got a short shelf-life. Trust graduates from state colleges, they won't know what a hell a paradigm is, or why the hell it shifted, but they'll out drink the enemy, and that's really all that counts in a first rate negotiation.

It's all starting to come together isn't it?

The hangover has not fully finished its life-cycle. At home your wife is amused with you. She'd rather not be but can't help herself. She doesn't want to *see* you pie-eyed, but as an abstract it has a certain boyish charm. She wants you to know that you can still get weird from time to time, but just doesn't want you to do it around *her*. And when she heads off with the girls to Nashville, don't be a dick.

The next day, after a few teeth brushings and relegating the dominant cave-man quality to just below the surface of your skin, you've fulfilled her expectations of what a man should be. Which was mighty nice of you, don't you think?

From the pleasant laziness of Taoism to the intense introspection of Buddhism to the oblivion of Nihilism, the hangover is the crossroads of the world's philosophies. The hangover makes you a better person.

In Iceland they have a word for it. I have neither the time nor the inclination to learn what that word is, but they've got to have one.

ACKNOWLEDGMENTS...

Are always a dubious honor in a book like this. Over the years I've forgotten where I ● ● ● picked up some pieces of information or lore, even if I can remember where I confirmed it. If I left you out, the next one is on me.

Bruce Van Wyngarten of *The Memphis Flyer*, gave me a spirits column, and much of that copy has shown up here, if in a very altered form. I've spent time discussing cocktails with Kevin Keogh of Bar Keogh, and DJ Naylor of the Celtic Crossing. Master Distiller Tom Morris of Brown-Forman was a great historical resource for all thing bourbon and Kentucky. The same goes for Pat Demere and our Sunday chats over a Guinness. Thanks to Hank Ingram for showing me around his floating rickhouse, and letting me sample the "juice." I rambled elsewhere through bourbon *terra firma* with Jay Winsler, Cy Holmes, Sam Buckmaster, Hugh Mallory, Keith Renard and Scott Knowlton – and that's the way you get into the vibe of the thing.

My late little brother Bernie came up with the title, *Drunk as Lords*, after leaving the seminary but before opening a bar called Murff's, thus leapfrogging 12 million Catholics with a single career shift. My older brother Larry created the first Murffbrau and has refined the method into something wonderful. He made some mead to help with my research, but admitted that "it tasted like honey and despair."

David Seale, whom I met at Phi Gam rush party playing quarters (resulting in a 25 year joke involving Dick Cavett) has been my partner in crime in the 4717's *Drunk As Lords* podcast. Another friend from the same class, Josh Hammond of Buster's Liquors – as well as his manager Kathrine Fultz – have helped me find the odd, limited whiskey pick. Their wine guru, John Vego has for years pointed me toward good wine, even if he never knew what I was doing with the experience.

Mostly, my gratitude goes to the charming, long-suffering, good humored Mrs. M., there is literally no one with whom I'd rather have a cocktail.

ABOUT THE AUTHOR

Richard Murff is the author of *Pothole of the Gods: On Holy War, Fake News & Other Ill-Advised Ideas* in addition to three novels, *Haint Punch*, *Yellowcake* and *One Last Hour*.

Murff has sailed in national level regattas (and gotten creamed in the process), is not terribly coordinated, but once bluffed his way out of arrest in Istanbul and Benghazi on the same morning.

Founder of the 4717, he is an editor, ghostwriter and analyst. He has written about spirits extensively as well as foreign affairs, hunting and other ill-advised adventures. His work has appeared in *The Bitter Southerner*, *Delta*, *Memphis Flyer*, *American Spectator*, *Sail* and several others.

The mint julep cookie was created in his honor.

SELECT BIBLIOGRAPHY

Amis, Kingsley, *Everyday Drinking*, Bloomsbury USA, New York, 2008

Berk, Sally Ann, *The Martini Book*, Black Dog & Leventhal, New York, 1997

Clark, Oz, *The Essential Wine Book: An Indispensable Guide to The Wines of The World*, Fireside,New York, 1988

Cuppy, Will, *The Decline and Fall of Practically Everybody*, Dorset Press, New York, 1950

Crowgey, Henry G., *Kentucky Bourbon: The Early Years of Whiskey Making*, University Press of Kentucky, Lexington 2008

Forsyth, Mark, *A Short History of Drunkeness*, Three Rivers Press, New York, 2017

Hughes, Robert, *The Fatal Shore:The Epic of Australia's Founding*, Vintage, New York, 1988

Kanner, Joseph, "The Stomach as Bioreactor: When Red Meat Meets Red Wine." *Journal of Agriculture and Food Chemistry.* August 2008

Lukacs, Paul, *Inventing Wine: A New History of One of The World's Most Ancient Pleasures*, Norton & Co., New York, 2012

Percy, Walker, "Bourbon." *Esquire*, December 1975, pp 148-150

Rogers, Adam, *Proof: The Science of Booze*, Houghton Mifflin Harcourt, Boston, 2014

Wodehouse, P.G., *Jeeves and the Ties that Bind, Scribner Paperback, New York, 1971*